Don't Compete,

Don't Compare,

Don't Complain

CONFESS

Melvina Bryant

Don't Compete, Don't Compare, Don't Complain: Confess
Published 2025 by Regina Sunshine Global Network LLC

Copyright© 2025 by Melvina Bryant

Cover Design by Darshawne Wickerson
Edited by Charlotte Ehney
Edited by Pamelia Stanley
Photography by Roderic Wright/Modest Media, LLC

Paperback ISBN: 979-8-9862575-8-7
Ebook ISBN: 979-8-9862575-9-4

Bible references quoted from King James Version and 1599 Geneva Bible from www.biblegateway.com.

All Rights Reserved. No part or portion of this publication may be reproduced, stored in a retrieval system, or transmitted in any form or by any means - electronic, mechanical, photocopying, recording, or otherwise - without the express written consent of the author.

For information:

Regina Sunshine Global Network, LLC
www.ReginaSunshine.com

Table of Contents

Preface 4
Change 7
A Thought 11
Don't Compete! 15
Our Helper 19
Don't Compare! 24
Fear 31
Faith 37
Forgiveness 43
Don't Complain! 47
Success or Failure 54
Contentment 59
Determination 64
Joy 69
Character 73
Prayer 76
Confess 84
Citations 89
About the Author 91

Preface

This book is inspired by the **HOLY SPIRIT** through prayer. It is dedicated to anyone who desires to have life abundantly. **Jesus** said that He **"came that we might have life and that more abundantly" (John 10:10).** The word **might** makes the implication we may or may not obtain life abundantly. If we desire, we can obtain an abundant life because Jesus came that we might have it.

This book is a tool for acknowledgement so we can recognize that we do speak words that are not of life and that we need to change the way we speak daily. It is intended to challenge us to choose words that produce life, to make confessions according to the impressive Word of GOD, and to refrain from speaking words that cause us to compete, compare or complain.

This book is designed to help us sow the seeds that will allow us to reap abundant blessings by changing what comes out of our mouths. It is written as an aid to change the way we speak. It is intended to be a guide to assist us in living a life of confessions so that we will speak life to every situation.

This book is also written to both inform us of the powerful Word of GOD and to reiterate how it works with confessions. The Bible says let your words be few **(Ecclesiastes 5:2).** Only spoken words can be life changing. We must learn to let our words be few yet powerful words of life. We must speak and be assured that all things are possible to him who believes **(Mark 9:23).**

The Word of GOD is full of ordinary people who with few words made confessions, and their lives were changed instantly. In **2 Kings Chapter 4**, the Shunammite woman went to Elisha after the death of her son. She spoke with few words regarding this situation saying, **"It is well"**, and her son was revived from the dead. In **Genesis Chapter 22**, Abraham spoke with words of faith. **"Abide ye here with the ass; and I and the lad will go yonder and worship and come again to you."** Although he was obeying GOD in attempting to sacrifice his son, Abraham's faith produced different results. GOD provided a sacrifice for him. With faith, Abraham spoke a confession that his son would return with him from the mountain.

The centurion spoke with few words to Jesus. **"Speak a word and my servant will be healed" (Matthew Chapter 8).** His servant was healed in that hour. The woman with the issue of blood also spoke with few words. **"If I may touch but his clothes, I shall be whole" (Mark 5:28).** As soon as she put action to her words, she was healed.

We speak words daily, but do we realize how powerful the words are that we speak? Words obtain life as soon as they are released into the atmosphere. Not only will we have to give an account of them, but we must live with the manifestations of the life that our words produce. Therefore, we must learn to speak powerful, positive words that will shape and reshape our lives.

We have an opportunity to choose what we decide to say. **"Out of the abundance of the heart the mouth speaks" (Matthew 12:34). "The heart is deceitful above all things, and desperately wicked: who can know it?" (Jeremiah 17:9).** We must change our hearts so that we can speak effective words. In **Jeremiah 17:10**, GOD says He searches the heart and the mind and gives to every man according to his ways and according to his doings. It is easy to be condescending and ill-willed. It is also easy to be positive, uplifting, and encouraging. We must speak about life in a world that is filled with so many defeating challenges. If we speak to circumstances and situations that we encounter with positive words, we will be victorious in every aspect of our lives.

Let us not be people who compete with others in society to set our own worth. Let us not compare by measuring our lives with the lives of others. Let us not complain as if GOD does not know what is best for us. But let us confess the changes we would like to see manifested in our lives.

Let us confess that we are more than conquerors and that we can do all things through Christ which strengthens us **(Romans 8:37, Phil 4:13).**

Let us examine why we choose to compete, compare, or complain. We will look at our reasons and see what the Word of GOD says. We will correct our actions so that we will have a starting point for change. After careful examination, we must adjust and begin to confess greater outcomes for our lives. If we are to produce change, we must begin with our confessions.

Change

Whenever GOD wanted to see change, He spoke it into existence. He said let there be, and change came about from the words that He spoke. We are spiritual beings made into the image of GOD, and that same authority is within us. We are Kings and Priests. When we speak, we make things happen. We generate change when we speak words that are positive or negative. We also generate change by our actions and reactions.

Sometimes we base our lives on the way people treat us. And sometimes we live our lives based on what people say to us. We want people to like us. We want to make friends and have loved ones. We change to satisfy others. We change our hairstyles. We change our attire to keep up with the trends. We may not like new hairdos or new clothes, but we do not want to be left out of social relationships or be unaccepted by our peers. We should be making changes to reflect our own personality or making changes that put us in line with the will of GOD. Our goals in life should be about having a life that is both meaningful and satisfying. Things do not always work out the way we hope or the way we plan. No matter how hard we try we cannot please everyone. Sometimes we cannot please ourselves.

We can have a spirit of indifference or apathy, which is an "I don't care" attitude. Situational apathy is caused by difficult circumstances according to the *JED Foundation* of Boston, Massachusetts. The Foundation states that *all forms of apathy that we express can be characterized by feelings of indifference or emotional numbness towards aspects of life.* To feel indifferent means that I do not care one way or the other. I am not positive, and I am not negative. I just do not care. Sometimes, feeling that others do not care for us can cause us to not care for ourselves. It creates a poor self-image and can lead to depression or suicidal tendencies.

I first began to experience adversity in grade school when I was bullied. The kids said mean things to me all the time. I lived in a single parent home with five siblings. My mom could not afford to purchase clothes and shoes for us. I was the fourth child and wore hand-me-downs each year.

My response to those bullies was to adopt an "I do not care" attitude. It became my favorite thing to say I don't care. You do not like me? I do not care. Do you want to come against me? I do not care. I wanted others to think I was stronger than they expected, and nothing they said would hurt me. I said I do not care to numb the pain, to relieve the embarrassment, and to conquer the fear. Actually, I really did care. I said I did not care to feel like I was in control. I said it to feel like I was not sad, depressed, or alone. I said it because I wanted to take away their power to make me afraid. It was my way of fighting back; my pride compelled me to put up a shield. I thought it was a great defense.

It was not indifference; it was fear. The fear of being confrontational, the fear of not having friends, and the fear of not being accepted because of financial situations. But it was all a lie. And I made up my mind to be honest with myself. I wanted people to know who I really was. Therefore, I made a change. I told myself I would never say those words again, and I have not.

When we **compete** with others, we subject ourselves to the lives of others based on the things that we think are important. We look at their lives and try to duplicate their lives. We adjust our lives to make us feel as if we are better than those we compete with. We lock ourselves side-by-side in someone else's category.

When we **compare** our lives with the lives of others, we concentrate on their lives more than we concentrate on our own lives. Therefore, we stay in a stagnant state. We are not moving forward nor are we moving backwards. We are just standing still. Any movement is better than standing still. Anywhere other than backwards is progress. Comparing our lives with the lives of others is to suggest that GOD is unfair and that we are not getting what is due to us. We imply that our lives do not measure up to the lives of others. No change can occur because we are blessing the fruits of another.

When we **complain,** we speak negative to the blessings of GOD. We speak words that will not produce good fruit in us. We speak against GOD and His wisdom for our lives. GOD can use everything that we go through to create a more positive and prosperous person in us. If we are thankful in all things, GOD can show forth His glory. Because we are impatient, we do not see our challenges as the other side of victory. We begin to compete, compare, and complain. But if we can only begin to confess those things that we have been assured of in the Word of GOD, we will begin to see change.

I stopped speaking the words "I don't care" because I did not want to live a lie. I admitted to myself how much I really cared about issues of life. Truthfully, I was afraid of the confrontations, so I put up a wall of falsehood. I began to confess to myself that my life was too meaningful to disregard any aspect of it. I was not going to live in a box. I not only confessed the change, but I also made steps to live the change.

When we begin to confess according to the Word of GOD, we begin to see the changes. We experience those things exceedingly and abundantly more than we imagined them to be. Our confessions are based on our faith, and we begin to believe in the things that we speak. We do not just speak words. We speak boldly and make our confessions with authority. We see the changes happening in our lives. With motivation, we continue to confess more change.

The Bible mentions that if we decree a thing it shall be established unto us **(Job 22:28)**. To make a decree means to order, command, or decide something. A King makes a decree, and it is set up among the people. It is implemented and strict penalties await anyone who defies the decree. When words are released into the atmosphere, they become active and produce manifestations.

Words have power, and they can produce either death or life **(Proverbs 18:21)**. Power can be described as the energy that takes life from words that are confessed. We must be careful of the words that we speak. If we have an expectation that something great will happen to us, we must speak the words that bring about that action. If we do not expect remarkable things to happen, we will say negative words that produce negative reactions.

If we continue to complain that life is not fair and to compare our lives with others so much that we begin to compete socially or economically with them, then we will not realize that GOD made provisions for us all. What GOD has prepared for us is not always associated or connected to the lives of others. Moses' life was not connected to his siblings; he was the only one that his mother placed in the Nile. David's life was not connected to his brothers; he was the only one fighting wild animals and the only one anointed to be king. Paul's life was not connected to the other disciples. He was the only one who was blinded in order that he may see. With confessions, we can speak the blessings of GOD into our lives.

Jesus told His disciples to speak to the mountain **(Matthew 21:21)**. The mountain represents the circumstances in our lives. The mountain can be a long-suffering illness, financial difficulties, or whatever various circumstances that we meet in our lives. He wants us to confess even though the mountain looks bigger than us, and it is in the way of our progress. We can say that it is no longer an obstacle. Although the mountain still exists, we believe that it no longer hinders us. Thus, we will neither be distracted nor halted by its existence because we confessed that the mountain is far away from us.

The bullying continued. The adversity remained consistent and so did the confrontations. What changed was I no longer feared any of it. It became normal to me, and I became stronger. I no longer had to pretend. I no longer had to think of ways to hide my fears.

The process of change starts with a thought. If we have a thought for change, then change will come. We begin to make changes when we think differently. We change the way we think with just a thought. One thought can begin to produce changes that will bring about a life full of confessions.

Father, the vision of change has been written very plainly. May the reader become the runner so that positive confessions can be manifested. Even if the vision shall tarry, it will not lie. It shall happen in Jesus' name. Amen.

A Thought

Webster describes a thought as any mental or intellectual activity involving one's subjective consciousness. Thoughts can have ideas and imagination or an arrangement of ideas. Without getting into the complexities of the brain's behavior or functions as it relates to thought, let us reflect on thought from an elementary view. We can all agree that we have thoughts. Thoughts are good and bad. Our thoughts are our own and can only be shared if we want. The Holy Spirit is the only one that knows our thoughts **(1 Corinthians 2:10-11 and Daniel 2:29).** What we think and how we value our thoughts in our everyday lives determine the words we speak.

Our thoughts have power just as our words have power. We must be careful what we think about. While we may not figure out every thought that enters our minds, we must decide which thoughts to discard and which thoughts we give life to. We must also decide which thoughts we cast down. Sometimes our thoughts are far removed from us. We have imaginations and ideas that come to us during the day, and we sometimes wonder where those thoughts came from.

We may think of the craziest things sometimes, but we must realize that thoughts are just suggestions. The word of GOD tells us to cast down imaginations and bring our thoughts into obedience. **Casting down imaginations, and every high thing that exalts itself against the**

knowledge of GOD and bringing into captivity every thought to the obedience of Christ (2 Corinthians 10:5). Our thoughts must line up with the Word of GOD, and we should obey the Word. Anytime our thoughts are not lining up with the Word of GOD, we must cast our thoughts down.

I spent a vast amount of time thinking when I was younger. I was an observer and a thinker. I still am. In fact, I was in isolation for hours. I am not sure if all people who are thinkers are also loners. I remember just sitting very still and thinking deep thoughts. I did not know it then, but I later found out that I was meditating. I gained insight and foresight from my meditations. I began to write down the things I remembered that really stuck out to me and my personal awareness. Words became my friend. I did not speak much, but I wrote all the time. Poetry was my first love. Although when I wrote my first poem, I had no idea I was writing poetry. I was writing the things that filled my heart during meditation.

When we do not know what to think, we can refer to the Word of GOD. We have a guide on what to think, and the Word of GOD will give us power. It also gives us an opportunity. We must think about whatever is moral excellence. We must also think about whatever is positive and life changing that helps us to succeed. Whatever is of faith, hope and love, we must think about these things. Whatever pushes us to be the best that we can be, we must think about these things. We must think of things that produce good fruit.

To produce good fruit, we must plant good seeds. We produce words from our hearts not our minds. As we think, so we are. **For as he thinketh in his heart, so is he (Proverbs 23:7).** What we think about enters into our hearts, and what is in our hearts will determine what comes out of our mouths. **For out of the abundance of the heart the mouth speaketh (Matthew 12:34).** We must think about what we say before we say it. Everything we think is not the most popular thing to say. Our thoughts can cause us to compete, compare, and complain. We need thoughts that will cause us to confess the positive outcome that we wish to see manifested in our lives. We must check all thoughts and make mature decisions about each one of them. We must not let everything we think guide us. We must not let the pressures of life and the challenges we face cause our thoughts to be our voice.

After acknowledging I was lying to myself and others when I said I did not care, my thoughts turned more to the things I did care about. I began to care about how my words and actions would make others feel. I knew I had to speak positive words to others after I confessed how the words of bullies made me feel. I did not want anyone to feel the way I felt, so I began to speak up when I saw others saddened by the words of a bully.

We must do as King David and ask GOD to create in us a new heart and renew the right spirit that we need to positively use every second of the day **(Psalms 51)**. The Spirit will lead us to be successful in this life. We have the power to conduct all things with the help of the Holy Spirit. When the Spirit leads us, we are called GOD's children **(Romans 8:14)**. We are successful when we are counted as one of GOD's children. When we are GOD's children, we become in his likeness. We begin to want the things of GOD. We no longer seek the riches of this world. All the riches of the world are not more valuable than knowing our heavenly Father and knowing His tender mercies. There is nothing in this life that can compare to the wisdom and the love that GOD gives. We can change the way we think and the way we speak if we want to. Nothing hinders that change except us and our decision-making efforts.

We think all day long about what we will do next. All we need is a thought to trust GOD. All we need is a thought to speak positive words. All we need is a thought to change our lives. A thought can shape our conversations, our actions, and our progress. Can a thought change a thought? Can we change a negative thought into a positive thought? Can we change a thought of fear into a thought of victory? Can we change a thought of defeat into a thought of determination? Can we change a thought of depression into a thought of motivation? Yes, we can, and with a thought we can change a frown into a smile.

We can change a thought before it becomes something we compete, compare, or complain about. We can change a thought into a confession and believe that we will receive whatever we say. We can change a thought of worry into a thought of prayer, a thought of hate into love, and a thought of unkindness to kindness. We all must control our thoughts; no one can do that for us. While others can make suggestions, it is up to us to decide the outcome of our communication based on our thoughts. We must control what we think about so that it will not lead us to compete with others. Competing with others is not wise and does not produce good fruit. We are here to help one another to make life pleasant for us all. We must not think of things that cause us to compare. We compare our lives with others when we feel disappointed about what someone receives; we think that others receive greater things than we do. And we begin to compare apples to oranges. The favor that we receive from GOD is not for now, it is for later. It is for helping others. We do not look at the things that we have received and are grateful. Instead, we covet what others have.

GOD has a greater plan, and we do not always see the end results at first. Therefore, we must trust GOD and not compare our lives with others. Comparing leads to complaining, and complaining is like calling GOD a liar. It is like saying to GOD that He does not know what is best. When we complain, we speak negatively about our lives. We do not look at the good things that we have; instead, we focus on what is not going well. We make a list of every negative thing we can think of. Complaining can lead to disappointment, and disappointment can lead to depression.

As I grew into adulthood, I saw others obtaining blessings, gaining opportunities, and reaching their goals. I thought to myself *Lord, when will I get my blessings?* I focused not on their accomplishments, but on the timing. I would congratulate them and say I am next. And sure enough, my opportunities started rolling in. I focused on GOD and his promises. I activated my faith on the manifestation of what I saw GOD doing for others.

Our thoughts can never measure up to GOD's thoughts. **For I know the thoughts that I think toward you, saith the LORD, thoughts of peace, and not of evil, to give you an expected end (Jeremiah 29:11).** GOD's thoughts are not our thoughts. GOD's ways are not our ways. We must remember GOD is for us not against us. What He does for others does not negate what He will do for us. GOD wants us to love one another. He does not want us to compete with one another. If we loved everyone as we are commanded to love, there would be no need to compete.

Father, we thank YOU for the opportunity to have thoughts and imaginations that can help us to make correct decisions. Thank YOU for YOUR word of clarity that teaches us to confess and speak to the mountain those things that will bring us into greatness. We speak life, and we speak progression in every area of our lives. We decree a word, and it shall be set up. We declare wholeness and balance in our lives that will cause us to have the right thoughts. We ask that YOU try our hearts and our minds and remove anything that is not like YOU. In Jesus' name, Amen.

Don't Compete!

Competition can be described as a process that measures the difference in performance, worth, or value. It can also be a tool that calculates data to decide a winner of different prizes or rewards. The dictionary defines the word compete as a verb that means **to strive to outdo another for acknowledgement; compete implies having a sense of rivalry and of striving to do one's best as well as to outdo another.**

I played different sports in the backyard with my brothers. They never taught me the objectives or all the rules of the games. They said to "hit the ball and run" or to "catch the ball and throw it". It was not until I joined the softball team at the recreation center that I learned the rules. Honestly, I was not a great player because I had not learned the rules. With coaching and practice, I saw myself improve. During the season, there would be a competition. There would be scheduled games with other teams that played better than our team. Soon there would be a championship game. I never really looked at the game as a competition because I was competing against myself to be a better player. This was my thought process. I know that it was my pride. Therefore, I never let the team know that I did not care about winning the game. I wanted to win for me, by not being the one to cause us to lose the game. I did not want to be embarrassed like when I first began to play. I used every opportunity to improve my game. Once I improved my skills, then it seemed like other players on the team began to improve as well. And we began to win.

There are multiple ways to compete. Merchants compete to get customers. Schools compete to get students. Salespeople compete to make sales. There is also competing in sporting and different events for entertainment purposes.

To be competitive is sometimes a way of life. But we should never measure accomplishments that are based on things such as wealth, individual property, social status, religion, education, or political achievements. It is okay to compete and compare differences, but not to live a competitive lifestyle based on **having a sense of rivalry.** A rival is to **have qualities or aptitudes that approach or equal to those of another: one of two or more striving to reach or obtain something that only one can have. It comes from the Latin word** *rivalis* **meaning one using the same stream as another.** To be competitive can be unhealthy if it causes extreme jealousy based on rivalry.

Joining the team and competing in the games gave me a roadmap for life. Always do your best to improve. Only look at your own shortcomings and not at others' shortcomings. Always be a collaborator who is willing to work hard.

Having a competitive attitude is not always unhealthy. We should all strive to always do our best not just to measure up to someone else's achievements, but for individual accomplishments that sustain life. We would all like to be acknowledged for our talents and successes. It is healthy to be competitive when it is well-disciplined so that it does not cause damage to others.

Competing becomes unhealthy when we begin to try to win just to prove that our accomplishments are better than someone else's. Competing for social status or to prove that one person is better than another may cause resentment. We become obsessive in our behavior by trying to show that we are better based solely on competing with one another. All accomplishments are great, and there is no human scale that defines achievements as being of greater or lesser importance. We let pride, price, popularity, prejudice, and plain ignorance measure the value of our accomplishments.

We should be praising one another for the achievements that we make and learning from one another so that we can improve our society. Competition should only be for sport or entertainment not for status quo or self-worth. We see in sporting competitions the levels of awards given to the fastest or the strongest. The trophy or the prize is given to the athlete who excels in all requirements for a timed event. The fastest runner wins the medal. But in the race of life, the victory is not given to the swift or to the strong. It is given to the one who endures or holds on to the end **(Ecclesiastes 9:11)**.

Through all the challenges of life, we experience success and failure. How we manage these challenges is a reliable assessment of whether we will achieve goals. The desire to be classified as the best and the insatiable hunger to obtain more can become a competitive spirit. That spirit or competitive desire may soon turn us into people who complain. The rivalry spirit will escalate when we compete and do not attain the goals we want. We may feel that we did not win the prize we desired because of an unfair situation. We start whining, complaining, and losing focus on why we started competing.

Competition can also be fueled by anger and jealousy. We sometimes let our emotions get entangled causing bitterness and resentment. This is when competition is not good. If we must be competitive, let it be a rewarding outcome and not a situation that stirs up strife towards another. Competitive behavior can destroy relationships. Some people thrive on a wager or setting up different circumstances to prove they are greater, that their ideas are the best, or their way of doing things is better than others. There really is nothing to prove because ideas are great, and it takes diversity to make multiple ideas greater. There is no way to really decide which ideas are the best. It may be that there is a great idea that fits the circumstance for the time being, but that is not a sign that other ideas are not equally as great. We must be willing to accept all ideas and build on them. What one idea lacks, the other idea can enhance thereby making all ideas great.

We learn and grow from each other, and we can flourish by implementing our ideas with others. That is called culture, and it leaves no room for competition. The desire to outdo others is a carnal way of living. If we do not control it, then it may one day control us. It can also lead us into comparing, complaining, and into depression instead of confessing. GOD has supplied the help we need to succeed in this life. It is up to us to receive help. The Holy Spirit, our teacher and guide, is a very present help whenever we need Him **(Psalms 46:1).** With the help of the Holy Spirit, we can mortify the deeds of the flesh from competing in unhealthy ways **(Romans 8:13).**

Father, we thank YOU for the differences that we share and how YOU have made us all so unique. Father, teach us how to share our differences with one another in positive ways. Lord, teach us to value our gifts as well as the gifts that YOU have given to others. Let us show with kindness that we are all special in our own individual ways. Father, teach us to understand that we are made in YOUR image, that all things come from YOU, and that we are made for YOU. We are not our own, and we should not imbue our ideas with pride to display competitive emotions. Father, supply healing from within so that our nature would not be to compete just to prove that we want to substantiate ourselves. It is YOU who will judge in Jesus' name. Amen.

Our Helper

We live in a world where life seems so unfair for so many people. There are difficulties surviving from day-to-day. Yet for others, life seems so pleasant and surreal. Most people cannot imagine going without not only the necessities but the material desires that they value. Although one or two of us may experience hardships in our lives, it may or may not be tied to finances. Those who encounter difficulties with money may think that there are no other types of hardships. There is suffering from pain and disease, loss of loved ones, disappointments, and discouragements. The reality of a GOD who has no respect of person seems unreal in the eyes of people who face diverse hardships in life. The GOD we serve is truthful, and His mercy does last forever. We must look at mighty GOD and remember to take our eyes off circumstances and situations that seem bigger than we can handle. If we see our problems bigger than we see our GOD, we stay in a defeated state. But if we believe that almighty GOD is available to help us whenever we need Him, then we have the victory. **"GOD is our refuge and strength, a very present help in trouble" (Psalms 46:1).** Therefore, if we believe the word of GOD, we have no reason to be distressed with the difficulties of our present conditions. The GOD who is our strength and refuge is always there with us. When we are faced with adversities, we have choices that we can make to manage our circumstances. We can do nothing and have a pity party when trouble arrives. We can begin to worry about the issues and pay no attention to the solution. We can profess defeat and live out the problem instead of confessing that this too shall pass. Or we can try to manage problems within the limitations of our being. We can try to resolve the issues with emotions. Operating on feelings never solves anything. In fact, it may tend to make things worse, exemplifying what Jesus says in **John Chapter 15 "without me you can do nothing"**. It is GOD who has made us and not we ourselves. If we cannot rely on the one who has made us, then on whom shall we rely? Also, we can make the wisest choice and let the one who is more capable handle the situations for us. Jesus sent us a Helper. Our first inclination should be to make our request known unto Him. Jesus says that the Holy Spirit will comfort us. Instead of having a pity party, cry out for help. Jesus says that the Holy Spirit will lead us into all truth. Feelings are not facts. Hence, no matter how much we hurt there is help.

GOD is pleased to know that we recognize Him as our champion and that we depend upon Him one hundred percent because He is concerned about us. **"Casting all of your care upon Him for He careth for you" (1 Peter 5:7)**. GOD is not concerned about our ability to manage inconvenient situations. GOD tells Paul that **"My grace is sufficient for thee: for my strength is made perfect in weakness" (2 Corinthians 12:9)**. To almighty GOD, our strength is irrelevant. GOD gives us what we need to manage every situation. We can do so many wonderful things, but whenever situations get too big for us, we should be more than willing to give it over to GOD, the Almighty. For when we cannot, He can.

After my divorce, it was difficult raising a child alone. I worked dead-end jobs. Times were tough. I was robbing Peter to pay Paul. You know, not paying one bill this month to pay another and then doing the same the next month with other bills. It was overwhelming. This was one of my first faith trials. Right after I found a wonderful job and was starting to wiggle out of the month-to-month dance with my bills, I remember getting a call I will never forget. At 4:45pm in the evening, the power company called. Keep in mind the time. It was closing time for the power company. I spoke with the woman on the phone. She told me that if I did not pay my power bill of $215.85 by noon tomorrow, my power would be disconnected. Well, I must say that was one of the strangest calls I ever received from the power company. I knew that I had the money. I could be there at 9:00 am when the power company opened the next day. And I responded with this information to the woman on the phone. The next day, I was promptly at the power company to pay my bill of $215.85. The call came the day before, at the closing of the power company, and I was at the power company the next day when the doors opened.

What happened in between the opening and the closing? My Helper had stepped in. When I reached the counter (oh, do not let me leave this part out!), the bill was delinquent for 2 months. I was relieved that I was able to pay the full amount of $215.85 without doing the bill dance. Now, imagine how I reacted when the woman looked up my information and told me I did not owe a bill. She says that the bill for $215.85 was paid and that I had a $50.00 credit on my account. I was in shock. I almost tore up the power company; I was thanking GOD and dancing all over the place. I felt like Mary, the mother of Jesus. How can this be? Something miraculous had happened from the closing of the business to the opening of the business the very next day. There was no dispute that I owed the money for the service. I went to sleep and woke up and my power bill was paid in full plus there was a credit to my account. I must say my faith increased from that moment. I asked other people had they ever received a call like that from the power company. No one had. I say that to say this, although I had the money, I was not sure when I was going to pay the bill. In other words, I did not feel the urgency to pay the bill. My power had been off before. I mentioned the dance with my bills I was doing. Sometimes the music was not right, and the dance did go well at times. The reason I needed to pay right away was because my new job was at night. I had a young daughter who had never experienced being in a house all alone with the power off. My Helper was looking out for me and my daughter. All things concerning me He perfected.

Challenging times can lead us into despair. We think that all is lost, but before we give in to circumstances, we need to realize that the Holy Spirit wants us to tag Him to jump into the battle for us. Then we can rest assured that the victory is won. So many times, the word of GOD gives us the ingredients that we need to make our lives more understandable. The word declares that **"in all thy getting get understanding" (Proverbs 4:7)**. We must understand that GOD has given us everything we need to survive in life. **"According as His divine power hath given to us all things that pertain unto life and godliness, through the knowledge of Him and hath called us to glory and virtue" (2 Peter 1:3)**. We must understand that **if it had not been for the Lord on our side** where would we be **(Psalms 124:1)**?

The reason so many of us do not know that we have everything that we need is because the understanding of it is given by the knowledge of Him. If we have no knowledge of Him, we cannot understand His word. Not understanding the word will make tough times seem unbearable. But if we understand in Him, Christ who is the word of GOD will allow us to **"live, and move and have our being" (Acts 17:28). And he is a very present help in times of trouble (Psalms 46:1)**. There is nothing that He will let defeat us. If we use our understanding of the Word, we can walk in confidence, and then we will obtain enough faith to confess. By confessing the word of GOD, we can move mountains into the sea **(Mark 11:22)**. We can speak to dry bones, and they will live **(Ezekiel 37:4)**. We can defeat the power of the enemy **(Luke 10:19)**. But if we do not understand that we have the power of life and death in our tongue, then we are defeated by our own passive behavior and misguided actions **(Proverbs 18: 21)**.

Words spoken are like arrows that hit the bull's eye every time. And we know that the bull has two eyes. We can imagine one eye of life and one eye of death. So, we can confess life, and we can confess death **(Proverbs 18: 21)**. If we love death, we will confess negative and dead words. But if we love life, we will speak positive words of hope. When Jesus was on his way to see Lazarus after the news of his death, His disciples questioned Him about going back to Jerusalem where His life had been threatened. While the disciples were speaking fear, Jesus began to speak faith. He said, **"is it not twelve hours in the day; as there are twelve hours in the night?" (John 11:7-10)**. He was saying to them if you can be afraid, then you can have faith. If you run in fear, then you will stumble because you have no light. But if you walk in faith, then you have the light, and it will keep you from stumbling. The light is for illumination. It helps us not only to see what is hidden in the dark, but it also helps us to be able to obtain insight so that we can begin to see the things that are hidden within. Those things must be illuminated with the Word of GOD. GOD can reveal to us those things that no man can show us. His Word will show us a new way of looking at things. With the help of the Holy Spirit, we can see how to be grateful for all things. We can appreciate how GOD has supported us, and we will not compare our lives with the lives of others. Comparison is like the total sum of equality. To compare one thing with another, there must be exactness or else the comparison is not conclusive. We are all made differently, and therefore, no comparison is relevant.

Father, I thank YOU for the understanding that comes from the knowledge of Christ that we live a life that is triumphant when we confess truth. Father, increase our understanding that we may know how to confess YOUR word with wisdom and power. Thank YOU for being our helper in times of trouble and for defeating what tries to defeat us. May we forever confess YOU as Lord and Savior. In Jesus' name, we pray. Amen.

Don't Compare!

Comparing is to stand side by side in someone else's category. We must always be outstanding. To compare **means to hold something or someone up against another**. To compare **is to liken unto or to show similarities and differences**. Comparisons are made each day for adequate and inadequate reasons.

There are unusual types of information that can be obtained from comparisons. For example, specific information can be analyzed for experiments, to prove theories or to compile statistics. There are also comparisons of past events with present situations to identify patterns or phases.

The dictionary describes the word compare as "to examine the character or qualities of; as of two or more persons or things; for the purpose of discovering our resemblances or differences" **(Webster's *Revised Unabridged Dictionary*).**

We can compare many things and qualities. We sometimes compare demographic data for the census and other reports to understand the status of different groups of people around the world. We compare cultural differences to learn about traditions and traits of a people. These are positive reasons to use comparisons.

There are also negative reasons that we compare. We compare one another because of our education, race, material substances or financial wealth. These types of comparisons are only used to find the worth of one human being in comparison to another. There are people who think they are superior beings. But all are made of flesh, and there is no good thing in the flesh **(Romans 7:18 and Romans 8:8)**. All have sinned and come short of the glory of GOD. None do well all the time, and none seek after GOD to obey him continuously **(Romans 3:10-12)**. If we must compare, let us use GOD as our example. GOD is the measuring device to compare against humanity **(Isaiah 46:5)**.

GOD never said that one man was greater than any other. There is no mention in GOD's Word that a culture on the run from another culture automatically makes the fleeing culture of royal descent. GOD creates all humankind. If you are mistreating what GOD has created, you are not loving as GOD commanded. There must be a stiff penalty to any culture who disobeys GOD so willingly and without fear.

To compare in this way is useless because GOD has no respect of person. No one's value in life is decided by things. There are different varieties of people. All are unique. We are all different but there are things that make us the same. GOD made us all in His image, and He formed us from the dust. **"And the Lord formed man of the dust of the ground and breathed into his nostrils the breath of life; and man became a living soul" (Genisus 2:7).**

We are all made for a specific purpose. GOD had a plan in mind when He decided to make each of us. I alone know the plans I have for you, plans to bring you prosperity and not disaster, plans to bring about the future you hope for **(Jeremiah 29:11 GNT)**.

With the mind of GOD, all things are possible. We are made different. If all of us were the same, the world would lack multiplicity. As humans, we rate things to find worth. We try to rate sins. We compare certain sins so that in our own minds some are more shameful. But GOD does not rate sin because all sin carries the same punishment – death. **"For the wages of sin is death" (Romans 6:23)**. GOD does not compare sins, nor does he compare people. GOD has no respect of person. He deals with us according to our faith levels. If we want to succeed in life, we must not spend time comparing ourselves to others or vice versa. Paul wrote to the Corinthian

Church that it is not wise to compare yourself with others; it is not enough to measure against **(2 Corinthians 10:12)**.

Before I started walking in faith, I remember telling the story of my marriage. I mentioned all the negative things that my ex-husband had done. I told everyone who would listen. I wanted to let everyone know how terrible my marriage was and why I had to get a divorce. I wanted to compare my life with all I had been through to the life of my ex-husband with the things he brought upon himself and the marriage. One day, someone asked me how long I stayed with my ex-husband before I decided to leave. I did not realize it at that moment, but that was a loaded question. I responded that I stayed for ten years. While I was comparing circumstances with situations, GOD showed me that I had to take a long, hard look at myself. I wanted to cast a dim light on my ex-husband and his actions, but I could not do that without shining a brighter light on myself. I had to ask myself questions. If the marriage was so terrible, why did I stay? Ten years is a long time. What was I saying about myself while trying to speak negatively about my ex-husband? I did leave over five times, but the familiar sometimes seems better than the unknown. I was looking at the mistreatment, but I was not looking at why I allowed it to continue.

It is not good to measure one with another because we are all different. No two can be alike. It is not a clever idea to compare the accomplishments or failures of others. Comparing ourselves with others will develop into competition. There will always be a plan to strive higher than the others in all type of competitions. Individuals are not given talents to compete against one another. Diversity is for helping one another. Competing to prove one is superior to the other can cause a lack of care and concern for one another **(Political campaigns)**.

No one wants to trust others because of the need to compete. No one is willing to rely on the other, and no one takes responsibility for the concerns of one another. We begin to live in a world of self-gratification. Superiority is measured by how the value of our material possessions exceeds that of our neighbors. Instead of using our educational background and social conditions as competitive devices against one another, we need to use them as resources to help one another.

Life progression should be decided by the ability to shoulder responsibility and not by how we measure up against one another. Sometimes we do not want to carry the weight of our responsibility. If we do not carry the responsibility to progress our lives, we can become fruitless. We become like the fig tree. If we have not produced fruit and it is the season to produce, then we become useless.

When I was comparing my life to my ex-husband's, I was not open to producing the lifestyle that GOD had chosen for me. I was living as a victim. I was living as a rejected wife. I began to compare all the support he received while he was working through the broken pieces of his life. I thought that I should have gotten all the support, but I got none. I became bitter because I stayed focused on raising my daughter and he did not. I felt as if his family did not love our vulnerable baby because they had the means to provide for her but did not offer any support. I felt alone. His parents knew of their son's struggle with drugs. He received so much love and support from them when he went to rehab. But they gave no support to his child.

Although I was hurt and confused, I began to stop feeling sorry for myself. I had a little girl who needed me. I no longer obsessed on the non-support. I focused on being a mother. I started to see that GOD had so much to offer. My life shifted from struggle to survival. I decided not to compare my life with anyone. I began to live. I was being equipped with the knowledge and understanding of GOD as my provider. I saw how I would be able to provide without any help from family. I realized that GOD was on my side.

When we are needed and we have no fruit, GOD wants something from us that we have not produced; nothing is hindering us from producing except us. If GOD comes to us looking for what He expects us to have and we do not have it, then we can be cursed like the fig tree to never bear fruit again and wither away **(Matthew 21:19)**. If we do not produce or reproduce, then ultimately, we may die without reaching our full potential.

For example, a newborn baby has a responsibility. His responsibility is to receive milk. While the mother has the responsibility to wean, it is the baby's responsibility to receive the milk to progress to the next level of life. **Adequate food consumption at an early age is vital for an infant's development**. If the baby is unable to meet that responsibility, the baby fails to progress in the first stages of life. If that baby does not consume the milk, the baby's bones will not grow and develop the muscles that are needed to become mobile. The bones will not fulfill the responsibility of strengthening the muscles and may cause the organs to begin to shut down. But if the baby shoulders the responsibility and receives the milk, the baby can move on to the next level of responsibility. The baby will be healthy, and the next level of responsibility will be mobility because the bones are stronger.

Each of us must accept our responsibility for growth in both the flesh and in the spirit. Our progression will change how we look at others. We will focus more on our own potential instead of comparing our lives to others.

The word of GOD speaks against comparing ourselves to one another, stating it is an unwise thing. **"For we dare not make ourselves of the number or compare ourselves with some that commend themselves: but we measure ourselves by ourselves, and comparing ourselves among ourselves, are not wise"** (2 Corinthians 10:12).

Most would not even dare to compare material things to substantiate worth. If someone cannot afford the same material things, then the thought is that one person's worth is greater than the other. GOD does not want us looking down on anyone or looking up to anyone because of material wealth. GOD blessing us usually means that it is our season, or it is the manifestation of our faith at work. GOD responds to His word and to our faith.

If you are a parent of more than one child, you realize each child has different needs. You are aware of the needs of each individual child, and you stand ready to meet every need. But you may not be able to manage each need all at once. You may have to decide which need is greater or which will be managed first. The most important thing is that you do not love one child more than the other. However, because of a greater need, one child's manifestation happens before the others. This is the same way that we must see the blessings that GOD has bestowed on others. When we see someone receive a blessing from the Lord, we should respond with joy and with the assurance that if GOD did it for them, He will also do it for us.

We cannot compare what the Lord does for one individual to what He does for another. Sometimes to receive a blessing, we must be prepared. The Lord will prepare us for the blessing, but the amount of time of the preparation will decide when the blessings will be bestowed. If GOD is trying to do something in our lives and our flesh is resisting, then the blessing will be delayed.

We must never compare ourselves with others especially when it involves the work of GOD. We are all made in the image of GOD. But most importantly, we are all the created beings of one who is mighty. He made us individuals. There has never been nor will there ever be anyone like you. Everything about you is unique: your face, your personality, your attitude, your faith, your character. Even babies produced with one labor are not the same.

As children of GOD, we are all promised an inheritance. The determination of our inheritance is based on whether we are children of GOD. **"For as many as are led by the Spirit of GOD, we are the sons of GOD" (Romans 8:14).** We must not look for an inheritance if the Spirit does not lead us because then we are not a son. We must not try to compare the inheritance of the son with that of an illegitimate (unlawful) child because the son has a greater inheritance. In fact, we inherited the same inheritance as the first born inherited. **"And if children, then heirs; heirs of GOD, and joint heirs with Christ" (Romans 8:17).**

Until we can yield ourselves completely, we should not look at the timing of the Lord's blessing on others. Just as you are made differently from others, your relationship with the Father is different. Although He loves us all collectively, we do not all have the same conversation with our Father. His love is the same, but the way He relates to us as individuals is diverse. We do not know how long it took others to yield, and of course, we do not know the mind of GOD. **"For as the heavens are higher than the earth, so are my ways higher than your ways, and my thoughts than your thoughts" (Isaiah 55:9).**

Sometimes we can pray, and GOD responds at once. Other times we will believe GOD for months, even years, and the manifestation of the blessing will still be held up. The duration and the determination of when a blessing will happen are up to GOD. Instead of comparing, we should pray with the spirit of confession. If we confess the word, we walk in truth. If we believe the Word, our faith will be put into action by confessing. To confess you must believe every word of GOD, even if it sounds impossible. Remember that whatever is impossible with man is always possible with GOD. If we are faithful, GOD can bring all things to pass. But if we are fearful, we walk in defeat. We become people who worry, and worrying is a sin. Fear is torment, and so we must have faith to walk out our confessions.

Father, we thank YOU for choosing such a diverse group to be YOUR children. YOU are not biased to any of us. YOU show us all YOUR love. Teach us to love our differences, to be motivated by others, and to draw strength from one another. Lord, we ask that YOU help us to celebrate that which YOU do in each of our lives so that we bring glory and honor to YOU and not ourselves. In Jesus' name, Amen.

Fear

Fear can be responding to a thought or an idea with predicted worries or concerns for something which may or may not happen. It is the act of hastily responding to situations that cause us to have regrets and emotional strains. Fear causes us to stress over problems which are perceived to have a negative outcome.

The lyrics of En Vogue's hit song "Hold On" include the line "Don't waste your time fighting blind minded thoughts of despair." In other words, do not let your mind play tricks on you! Fear torments us. We think that crazy things will happen, but the things we think will happen never actually do. If we can have thoughts of fear, we can have thoughts of victory, joy, and peace.

Fear is the unknown outcome that is believed to be detrimental. It is thoughts that compound past failures and present procrastinations to halt future endeavors. Fear is inward turmoil that causes bondage to our souls; it is the belief that destruction and afflictions are inevitable. Fear agitates us and causes us to imagine the outcome of a situation to be negative based on past circumstances.

I was fearful of failing in every area of my life. After so much failure, I thought that it was my destiny to fail. I was willing to try, but I had no support or someone always shot down my ideas, so I felt helpless. But one night during the middle of the week, I attended a conference. I was so tired.

I almost declined the invitation. As I entered the crowded event, even before I could find a seat, the speaker called me forward. I was told "GOD said no more failures." I jumped! I screamed! I howled to the moon! I did not know what reaction to have. It was great news, and I must say that it happened. Failure was like acne; it would not go away. It was a part of my life. It was a part of my mother's life; it was a part of my grandmother's life. But after that night, my life changed. Whatever I set out to do in my life, I was successful without support or having my ideas shot down.

I went back to school and earned my degree in Computer Science. GOD had already given me a job in corporate America before I received my degree. I was able to overcome my fears, which allowed me to have more faith, more love, and more understanding of a mighty GOD.

Fear encourages us to hide within ourselves and create a comfort zone that allows us to portray outward characteristics that may project other emotions. For example, a bully may have a fear of being embarrassed or being taunted by others; the immediate response to fear is to become a bully and not have to face shame or embarrassment. Another example of fear coming out as other emotions is when we are afraid of being lonely; we will make friends and do whatever it takes to please other people. We will endure friendships that are not safe or not emotionally stable to counter the fear of being alone.

I was always a "yes" person. I was so happy that someone thought me worthy of the asked task. I felt greatly honored to be asked to do certain things for certain people. At the time, I did not realize that it was co-dependency. I said yes without considering the size of the task. Then came the day I realized that I could not complete a certain task that was asked of me. I had always said yes to this person. So, when I said no I was treated with more disrespect than I had ever felt from another human being. Someone I admired, loved, and respected treated me coldly and disregarded my feelings. I was so shocked. Afterwards, it took me a long time to say "yes" to anyone other than GOD.

I cannot say that I had friends. I had associates. I had people who only associated with me because I supported them. Now that I think back on it, I allowed their behavior so I could feel like I belonged. This is so horrible. I did not want to be alone. But as I reflect on it, I was always alone. I accepted the way they treated me. I did not realize that others were rejecting me. I just wanted to please them.

A fear of failure will cause us to cease taking on different challenges because our minds are programmed to accept that we will fail. The fear of rejection will cause us to avoid involvement in relationships. The fear of anxiety will cause us to lose the desire to meet others or be remiss in social activities. There are all types of fears that can cause us to withdraw or refrain from normal activities; fear causes us to conceal the main phobias.

Fear causes us to try to win at any cost. The fear of not measuring up will cause us to spend every dime to acquire material possessions to achieve greater social status. We are driven by fear so much that we rearrange our lives to act like someone who can obtain materialistic objects just so we can feel secure. We are comparing ourselves to others, and the fear of not measuring up is devastating to us.

Sometimes, fear is the mental conversations that we have within ourselves. Perhaps it's the constant thought that terrible things will happen. It could be anticipating other people's negative reactions. Both of these can cause us to have fears that may never manifest. This causes us to withdraw rather than face fear. People who have a fear of flying constantly think about a plane crashing; they never imagine a safe and relaxing flight. Thoughts and behaviors give life to fear. If we change the way that we think about fear, it will disappear. The very thing that we fear will be the very thing that comes upon us. **For the thing which I greatly feared is come upon me, and that which I was afraid of is come unto me (Job 3:25).**

The spirit of fear as a living entity has a distinct existence -- meaning it has a power, a will, and a determination to compel and to draw. Fear is a force, a weakness, and a torment. Fear will make you go the long way home to avoid running into someone you think is going to cause you danger or embarrassment. Fear forces us to believe in the unexpected or in unimaginable things.

Procrastination is a form of fear. Whenever I have a big project, I begin to fear that I will not succeed. I prioritize other little projects over the big one. I make smaller projects into busy work. I feel justified to cling on to the things I know I can complete while running away from the important project because of the fear of failure. That is all it is -- putting off one thing to do another because I am frightened that I cannot do it. I now rely on GOD for everything. I ask GOD to help me even if I feel like I can do it. I'd rather lean on Him.

While fear is a significant factor in procrastination, it's not the only one. Procrastination can also be influenced by factors like poor time management, distractions, lack of motivation, and habit formation. Overcoming procrastination often involves recognizing the underlying emotions and beliefs (such as fear) and developing strategies to address them. This may include setting realistic goals; breaking tasks into smaller, more manageable steps; seeking support and accountability; and learning to cope with the fear of failure or judgment in healthier ways.

Fear has a compelling force. It will disable the power of those drawn to it. It weakens the ability to speak life and confess victory. It has the essence to cause a living being to progress into diverse stages. It is an evil spirit because it carries torment. There is no good progression when we fear. We do not move forward. We are still stuck in our fears.

Fear is a spirit, and it is not given by GOD. **"For God hath not given us the spirit of fear; but of power, and of love, and of a sound mind" (2 Timothy 1:7 KJV).** We say we trust GOD, and we believe that He is all powerful. Then there is no need to fear. If we are sure of GOD and His mighty power, there is no need to fear. The reason we fear is because we look at the natural realm. We use our senses to predict outcomes. We are drawn in by the results of past occurrences. The increase of fear is the decrease of love. There is no fear in love. When that which is perfect comes, it will cause fear to dissipate. It is like putting gasoline in our cars. What happened to the liquid substance? It has changed into a vapor that disappears the more we drive. The more love we share, the more fear will disappear. It will evaporate, and in time we will have no fear. No fear of circumstances or situations will hinder us. Love is a fruit, and there is no law -- meaning no limitation. We can love as much as we choose.

Looking backwards instead of looking forward causes us to fear. There are always going to be challenges in life. One must never live life as though we are defeated by circumstances. Instead of looking at the content of the situations, we should be looking at the greatness of our GOD. Fear is also the opposite of faith. If we can believe the worst, we can also believe the best. Fear says the outcome is unpleasant. Faith says the outcome is peaceful. The act of responding to fear is sin. Worrying and doubting gives life to fear. Trusting and hoping gives life to faith. Fear will choke out the desire to have faith. There can be no faith where there is fear, and there can be no fear where there is faith. The scale will tilt either one direction or the other. The two can never be combined. They are opposing one another.

Because of fear, people will always compare themselves to one another. We fear that we will never measure up to the standards of others. Or we fear that no one will see our good qualities because of the attention that is placed on another individual. We fear we will be rejected and overlooked or that our talents and abilities are too small to be valued.

Fear causes us to go out of our way to prove how great we are in comparison to others. Fear causes us to want to compete. People will be competing with an opponent who may never be aware that they are in a competition.

Fear can also cause us to complain about life based on what others have achieved. The fear of failure can cause us to point our fingers and be disappointed about the outcome of every situation in life. We may never see life's good intentions, never feel qualified, never accept compliments, and never stop looking over our shoulder. We will only see negative circumstances. Therefore, fear keeps us in opposition to positivity and to greater outcomes. Our first response will be to complain.

Complaining will not allow us to have positive confessions. Our confessions will be marked by fear. Consequently, we will speak words of death instead of words of life. Fear will cause us to confess only the darkness that is haunting us. We will not confess change or divine transformation. We will not believe in a greater outcome. Our minds are programmed to only think of those things that will continue to have us walk in fear. We must begin to renew our minds to think about positive outcomes and greater expectations. We must be ready to receive the favor of GOD. We must have the mental ability to refrain from our old habits and to develop current ideas that give hope for the future. Life is full of difficulties, but the energy that is spent on fear can be stored up for rejoicing. We can change our fears into faith by thinking different thoughts. The thought of gratitude can cause us to change our fear into faith.

Father, I thank YOU for that which shall come, the perfect love which casts out all fear because fear has torment. I pray for those who are bound by fear that they will be released from the spirit of bondage to fear and that they will take on the Spirit of adoption whereby we cry Abba Father. Abba Father, YOU are a very present help in times of trouble. Father, give us a plain path that would lead us into YOUR presence because, as King David declares, in YOUR presence is fullness of joy and at YOUR right hand are pleasures evermore. Lord, I pray that we would draw nigh to YOU as YOU would draw nigh to us, and we can receive the fullness of YOU. In Jesus' name, Amen.

Faith

Faith is the ability to believe GOD without fear or doubt. It is our confidence that we have a **Hero** who can defeat any circumstances. If we remove the letter "i" from the word "faith", we have f-a-t-h and we began to see the Father. If we rely on and trust the Father more than we do ourselves, we begin to run in faith.

Faith comes by hearing the Word of GOD. It also comes by doing what we hear. We must activate the Word as we hear it or as the Holy Spirit reveals it to us. We must hear more of GOD and His instructions for our lives than we hear from the media, relatives, coworkers, or ourselves. By listening to the Word of GOD, it begins to transform us. The Word of GOD is a transforming Word to change us, and faith is activated in us as believers through the Word of GOD. We respond to the promises of GOD through faith. Without faith, we cannot please GOD. With each year of experiencing the awesomeness of GOD, we must grow in faith. Faith is also a complex belief that can have different meanings depending on one's background and religious, moral, or personal perspective.

I did not believe in myself for a long time. I thought that people had to believe in me for me to believe in myself. I did not like myself for a long time. I thought that I would not amount to anything. I never had friends and family members that cheered for me, and I still do not. I learned to believe in myself from faith in GOD. I learned to love myself from having faith in GOD. I was curious how Abraham knew which mountain to climb. I wondered what would have happened to Issac if Abraham did not believe GOD for every action that he took. Abraham left his home with no idea where he was going. He had instructions, but they were vague. How did he know that his first steps were the correct steps? Did Abraham second guess himself about his own ideas and his own motives? He had already given one son away to the wilderness. Would he go back home without his son for a second time? He had learned to release when he took Ishmael and sent him away. Imagine how he must have felt turning away from his own flesh and blood not knowing what would become of Ishmael. Abrahma had twelve years with Ishmael, so he must have loved him and wanted to protect him. It was as if Abraham denied himself and whatever GOD told him he was all in.

Faith often refers to a strong belief in GOD. It involves trust, devotion, and a sense of conviction in the teachings, doctrines, and principles of a particular divine relationship. Faith is a spiritual or personal journey of seeking meaning and connection with something greater than us. This may or may not align with all religion, but can involve a sense of inner peace, or a quest for deeper understanding of life's mysteries. Faith can be a central quality of people's lives, guiding their moral and ethical choices and providing a sense of purpose and meaning.

I remember how easily I spoke with negativity; I spoke about how something would never happen. I thought it could not, and I never changed my mind about the negative way I saw it. It was so easy to relax in that mindset. I thought I was justified in never working towards the ideas because they would never work. I stopped brainstorming ideas because I had already convinced myself that they would not work. Not once did it occur to me to confess that this could actually happen. I think like that today. But how many of my future dreams or realities did I delay because of the mindset I had back then? Faith is virtue; it is a gift. Faith levels increase with maturity and life experiences. What we believe and how we practice our faith may change during our lives as we face different challenges or transitions.

There are processes that we go through that cause us to see GOD greater when we increase our level of faith. Therefore, it is helpful for us to increase our level of faith. We must be like Abraham, fully convinced that whatever GOD promised He is more than capable to perform **(Romans 4:17)**. We must know the promises of GOD to be persuaded by them. We must have an assurance that regardless of external circumstances GOD holds true to His Word. Our faith makes us righteous in GOD's sight. He judged Abraham's righteousness because of his faith. When we hear GOD's word, it produces faith. Faith is the only thing that pleases GOD because without it we cannot please Him **(Hebrews 11:6).**

Faith is personal. It changes one's beliefs and views. Whether or not faith "increases" can vary from person to person and depends on factors, including individual experiences, spiritual or religious practices, exposure to innovative ideas, and personal convictions. Every day our faith is ignited in a way. When we hear of a miracle that happened, we begin to have faith that a miracle can happen for us as well. When we hear about an excellent product, we desire to try it. When we hear about money making ideas that are successful, we want to rush out and try to achieve the same success. When we hear about different tragedies, we begin to take precautions so that the same fate will not befall us. We all have been given a measure of faith. **"According as GOD hath dealt to every man the measure of faith (Romans 12:3).**

The level of faith that we obtain will cause us to act or react to things differently. Our response to the diverse events in our lives prove faith or the lack thereof. Firsthand experiences, whether positive or negative, can play a significant role in the increase of faith. Positive experiences can strengthen one's faith. Facing and overcoming challenges or doubts can also lead to a deeper, more resilient faith, especially when you know that it was GOD that helped to overcome the adversities.

If we can respond with the definite assurance that all is well, we have activated our faith. The outcome is never subject to judgment or doubt. The outcome is a sigh of relief because the result is victorious no matter what the circumstance. We are one hundred percent assured that GOD can do that which is impossible for us to do. We rely on the formidable power of Almighty GOD. GOD is immutable. His attributes are unchangeable, but His methods are transforming.

Jesus says that we must have faith as a grain of a mustard seed. The grain is what is being stressed more than the seed; that is the tiniest part and is invisible to the naked eye. Yet, it has great significance in the seed. Jesus is describing a greater increase in faith. Just as the grain is connected to the earth to grow, we must be connected to GOD so that when planted our faith grows tremendously. A mustard seed is the smallest seed. It is about

2 mm and tightly packed so that there is no place for air. It is an herb. The grain does not remain at its weakest state but flourishes and produces more seeds. So, we shall accomplish the same with our faith. **And the Lord said, if ye had faith as a grain of mustard seed, ye might say unto this sycamine tree, and be thou plucked up by the root, and be thou planted in the sea; and it should obey you (Luke 17:6).**

We must develop our faith to withstand tough times. We must realize that our faith is on trial, but we are not **(James 1:2)**. When we walk in faith, we move in the authority of GOD. We speak and we believe that whatsoever we say we shall have it. For this reason, we do not have to compete, compare, or complain. We confess that we can believe GOD in any type of circumstance. **For verily I say unto you, that whosoever shall say unto this mountain, be thou removed, and be thou cast into the sea; and shall not doubt in his heart, but shall believe that those things which he saith shall come to pass; he shall have whatsoever he saith (Mark 11:23).**

We compete with others because we do not trust GOD for the blessings that He has designed for us. We look at others as if GOD has given them all that there is in life, and we are left with nothing. We do not give thanks to GOD, the one who is able to supply all our needs. He has more for us than our minds can imagine.

Whenever we compare or complain, we are not walking in faith. What we are displaying is a lack of trust in GOD. When we compare our lives with others, we are trying to be someone we are not. We are watching the lives of others and trying to fit our lives to match theirs. We cannot be what we were not created to be. We need to be grateful to GOD for the life we have.

We complain because we are not satisfied with the life that GOD has for us, as though we could carve out a better one for ourselves. We try to exemplify that we are in control and GOD is not. We stop thinking about the goodness of GOD and think on present activities through our five senses. We must begin to see GOD greater than what our thoughts can imagine. We must pray that GOD will increase our faith so that we can believe the impossible. We can declare a thing, and it shall happen. Therefore, we will not compete, compare, or complain; we will confess.

When we confess how remarkable GOD is to us, we are expressing faith and displaying our confidence. When we speak about those things that are not as though they are, we are working in faith. We must begin to realize that we must confess who we are, what we are, and whose we are. The most important thing that we can do to help ourselves is to believe in ourselves. When we believe in ourselves, we believe in the Almighty, the GOD who created us. And when we connect with His purpose, we become everything that He has made us.

Jesus told His disciples to **speak to the mountain**. That is confessing that trouble is no longer an obstacle. GOD says **call unto me and I will answer you**. That is confessing that we need Him. GOD says that **His strength is made perfect in our weakness**. When we confess that statement, we begin to conquer that which has held us bound. We only need to believe that GOD is greater than anything that is internal or external. We must increase faith and apply it to our lives daily. The words we speak are a progression of faith when we confess and then see the manifestations of what we say. There is impressive power in the confidence that is developed in activating our faith.

Faith progression is not an overnight phenomenon; it takes a developmental attitude to practice trusting in GOD and His every Word. Once we see the resulting miracles, we are increasingly excited to trust Him. GOD is pleased that we depend on Him, and he reveals more of his wisdom to us. In exchange, there is a confidence that can only be progressed gradually by a deeper desire to obtain more faith. Once faith is activated, there is nothing that can turn it off. There may be obstacles that cause us to waver in faith, but if we have it and we activate it, faith will work for us. There are measures of faith which means we must obtain faith a little at a time. We may have faith to believe that we will be successful in business, but that faith may not be enough to believe that we can be healed from a terminal disease. We must develop faith. The only way that we can obtain more faith is to be evaluated. The trying of our faith produces patience **(James 1).**

The patience that is produced is a peace that allows us to remain calm and let the transference of a greater faith begin. We must keep our faith at each level by remembering what has already been done. As we progress in faith, we are not only walking in liberty which helps us to grow stronger, but in faith which allows us to walk with others and help build up their confidence. We become a pillar and an encourager to speak boldly and mix our faith with the faith of others to see powerful manifestations. And because we activate faith, another measure of faith is gained.

As faith is acquired, it becomes a powerful way to use the authority and the liberty of confession. With a greater measure of faith, our confessions become bolder because we now are fully persuaded that we shall have whatever we say. We speak with confidence that says it is so. We know that what we say will manifest in its own timing. And we with patience will wait for it.

Faith works on both sides of confessing. It is what we hope for that produces the manifestation of what we desire. Faith comes by hearing of the Word, but it is also the evidence of things hoped for. What are we hoping for? Faith to hear, to speak, and then to believe. The equation is hearing, confessing, and believing that we will receive. It is not enough to have one without the other. If we hear but never confess or believe, then all we did was receive the word. Confess it, or no manifestation will result. Likewise, if we believe but never confess, there is nothing to produce. We must use all hearing, confessions, and belief. When we walk in all, we become stronger, our desires begin to change, and we develop the heart of GOD. A heart of GOD is a heart that loves and a heart that forgives.

Father, thank YOU for the spirit of faith. As we put more trust in YOU to believe all things, we will obtain another measure of faith. Let us hear YOUR word with simplicity and clarity because faith comes by hearing YOUR word. Father, we pray that YOU will keep us mindful to help others to obtain a greater level of faith by encouraging and inspiring them. Faith is the substance of things not seen. Help us Lord to work outside of our senses so that we will not limit our ability to obtain the measure of faith that YOU have for us. In Jesus' name, Amen.

Forgiveness

Forgiveness is excusing an offense and refraining from resentment or condemnation. It means to let go of all hurt and ill feelings as though the incident never happened. It means to get new boundaries to successfully relate without the idea of charging with penalties.

Forgiveness is a conscious and deliberate decision to release feelings of anger, vengeance, and retribution, and to instead offer understanding, compassion, and pardon to the person who caused the harm. Whenever we say we forgive, we must show forgiveness as well. We must not continue to bring up the situation or the circumstance to remind the person of the fault. We must be careful that we do not hold them in bondage for the pain that was once inflicted. To truly forgive, we must put ourselves into their position and imagine how we would desire to be forgiven had we committed the offense. We must not hold up caution signs when we encounter the offender. We must not reject the presence of that person; we acknowledge them with love and respect.

I have been guilty of this. I will not be angry, but I am always on alert. If we were once close, I can engage with the person who has hurt me, but I can never feel assured of resuming the same type of relationship we once had. For a stranger, I can forgive because I may never see that person again, and I am assured that whatever harm that they caused is something that may occur with others.

We must forgive as the Father forgives us. He does not recall our sins to us. **As far as the east is from the west,** *so* **far hath he removed our transgressions from us! (Psalms 103:12).**

My heart skipped a beat when I encountered someone I felt had done me an injustice. I had mercy and I had forgiveness, but I also had an alert. I immediately felt that I had to leave the room. I didn't want to be confused, ashamed or embarrassed by my reactions to things that would be said or done in that moment. For me, I needed to become invisible. I was not healed, but I was obedient. I cannot say that I wished the best for that person, but I didn't want to react with disdain. Neither did I want to feel like a victim. The timing was off, so I needed to leave that space for my healing. I needed to find a face that I could trust and go over to that person, not just for exclusivity, but also for strength to endure. I do not know if the person I started speaking to realized that they had become mediator in the moment. We are all humans, and we must be honest about our emotions. While I relied on my trust in GOD, I did not want to display any fleshly regrets. Basically, I knew I needed a little more time to process the offense to be healed. Although I knew I had forgiven because I was not upset, I was not ready for the encounter. No one can give a blueprint of the amount of time it would take for me to heal from the emotional damage that I suffered; however, that does not change that I must be obedient to forgive. It is not a prescribed method of forgiveness versus healing. Healing is in forgiveness. There is no heaviness, but there is still a hurt. And after timing, I forgot what the offense was and was able to be in the presence of that person again. Now we have a better relationship than before. It took time to heal, but forgiveness was necessary.

It is better to forgive than to hold an offense. Forgiveness is a process of emotional healing and moving on from the pain or hurt caused by the wrongdoings of others. It is abandoning negative emotions like anger, bitterness, and resentment. If we do not forgive, we are setting up a wall to become bitter and resentful towards others. These are the things that can cause us to compete, compare or complain. Having unforgiveness can also cause us not to walk in confessions. Jesus said, **"What things soever you desire, when you pray, believe that you receive them" (Mark 11:24).** Then Jesus immediately starts teaching on forgiveness in the next sentence.

Confessing and forgiveness are synonymous. Although forgiveness is about the well-being of the person who forgives, as it can lead to freedom from emotional stress, forgiveness is a personal choice. It does not require the wrongdoer to apologize or express remorse, although such actions can help the forgiveness process. It allows us to walk in obedience to GOD's word and just forgive. It may be a sacrifice to forgive, but **obedience is better than sacrifice.**

To forgive a person is to offer a new and fresh opportunity for them to make better choices. Unforgiveness allows the hurt to be relived, and to replay the event multiple times in our minds until we are satisfied that the person knows the extent of the pain they caused. We think that this will help us to heal. But all unforgiveness does is torment us. Unforgiveness torments us as a victim, but we are healed instantly when we decide to forgive. We also cease to speak on the offense. Faith must get us to this point. We are quick to say, "I forgive, but I certainly will not forget." To continue to relive the past pain is a state of stagnation. It is also a tormenting spirit of fear. There is a fear that someone will always hurt us. We will live our lives in a protective mode always being on guard to stop the offense before it occurs. But perfect love casts out all fear. If we love ourselves enough to heal, then we will love others enough to forgive.

Healing is not always an immediate process once we begin to forgive. When we decide to forgive, we are moving forward with our lives. To forgive means that we accept the misdeed, and we move on even if we do not get an acknowledgment of guilt. Even if we never get an apology, healing is the reward. Healing enables us to move on. We do hurt others, sometime unaware, and we need forgiveness. If we want forgiveness, we must learn to forgive.

Our greatest offense is to our heavenly Father. We are unfaithful, disobedient, and carnal. We are **drawn away after our own lust**. We are unfruitful and unproductive. We are not good stewards with our time. But GOD who is merciful is willing to forgive us, and He is so kind to not count it against us. If GOD can forgive us, who are we that we cannot forgive? He does not forgive us for us. **He forgives for His name's sake**. We must learn to be more like GOD and forgive others for our name's sake. It is for our name's sake that we have peace and sanity to have a better heart instead of a bitter one.

We confess that we are walking in liberty and that we will not let the pain of past hurts cause us to speak words of death. We choose to love as the Father loves us. Forgiveness is not for the person that wronged us; it is because we love our Father. We should not be looking for any rewards from the one we forgive. All our help comes from GOD. When we forgive, we do not compete, compare, or complain. We will not compare the deeds done to us against the deeds done to others. We will not take on a victimized spirit and always feel defeated because of the actions or reactions of others. We will not complain that we are always being mistreated by others and that no one loves or cares for us. We will not compete for the love of those who disrespect and continually mistreat us. But we will start to confess **that if GOD be for us who can be against us?**

If we begin to have positive confessions in our life, we will see changes at once. We confess that we walk in liberty and the spirit of bondage has been released from our lives. We confess that we are healed from emotional turmoil and heartaches. We confess that we walk in forgiveness and love. We confess that we are victorious. When we confess and believe in our hearts, we shall have what we say. So, we will not complain about the hurt, we will confess that we will have greater relationships.

Father, we thank YOU for YOUR love and YOUR kindness that forgives us and cleanses us. Thank YOU for showing us love and kindness and tender mercy. We are grateful that YOU love us despite ourselves. Teach us how to have mature love that casts out all fear. Lord, let us not continue to hold the offense against others that we may be healed. We speak to every situation that has caused us to be broken-hearted. We speak life to every situation that causes us to feel defeated. We confess that we are winners because all things work together for our good. In Jesus' name, Amen.

Don't Complain!

Webster defines the verb complain as "to give utterance to expression of grief, pain, censure, regret, to lament; to murmur; to find fault" (***Webster's Revised Unabridged Dictionary***).

We know that verbs are action words. For every action, there is a reaction. When we complain, we are confessing words that are negative and unappreciative.

We all have tough times, but we must be mindful that we have had wonderful times too. We did not complain that we were having too much of the good life and wanted it to cease.

Honestly, I learned not to complain because GOD did not give me another person I felt comfortable complaining to. Truthfully, GOD always had me be the encourager. I could not complain and try to edify others at the same time. GOD gave me enough grace to suck it all in and continue to minister strength to others while I was going through my trials. I could not complain because GOD showed me the power of HIS word and my confession of HIS word in prayer. GOD had me praying for others nationwide. I had to be tough. I had to stand and withstand. I had to be a pillar. I could not have cracks and be broken and torn down. I could not give the enemy access to my emotions while in spiritual warfare for others. I had to lift others. After praying for others, I saw how small my issue really was, and there was no need to complain. GOD gave me courage to know

HIM on another level. GOD gave me the power to pray for others, and that is how I learned to pray for myself. Nothing is too hard for GOD.

When we complain, we are confessing that GOD is unjust and unmerciful. We show that we have a lack of gratitude. We insinuate that whatever happens in our lives should only be to our satisfaction. GOD has a tremendous task. He oversees the universe. When we complain, it is as if we want GOD to drop all His concerns and cares for others and instantly rearrange life just to please us. We are demanding GOD to do for us what we are not willing to do for HIM.

Our loving Father is so kind and so willing to deal with our needs. But if He does not move fast enough, we want to manage the situation ourselves. And the first thing we begin to do is complain.

I reflect on Joseph whose brothers sold him into slavery but God elevated to power. I can imagine Joseph all alone in that pit. I can imagine it was cold and maybe damp. I can imagine the rodents and the stench. I can imagine Joseph crying and feeling despair. I can imagine him feeling like it was just a joke and he would get to go home soon. I can imagine Joseph accepting the fact that he would be cold and alone, and then praising GOD. I can imagine what it felt like to be lied on, and no one hearing his side of the story. I can imagine Joseph always doing his best, but never getting recognized for his efforts. I can imagine Joseph encouraging others while he was locked up, yet free. I can imagine him interpreting the dreams of others while living his nightmare. I can imagine Joseph seeing his family and feeling love instead of hate. I can imagine Joseph's tears as bitter and sweet.

We must all go through the Joseph experience. We can make it to the palace if we focus on God's transport method and endure. We must not focus on the problem more than the purpose or the plan. God knows the plan He has for us. We don't know the plan; it is not suggested to try and figure out the plan. If we trust the planner, the results will inevitably work in our favor. It is being content with the present situation while knowing that it will not change immediately and no amount of complaining will make it better. It is praising God that the circumstance are not worse and that victory is the cross.

Being grateful is an antidote for trouble. It says that no matter what happens I am still blessed. I am still precious in HIS sight. I can speak to someone else's dream when mine looks like a nightmare. I can go to sleep when the King wants to kill me and has sixteen soldiers guarding me. I can go to sleep in the lion's den. I can slay a giant.

Complaining is not a cross-carrying attitude. It is a weak, sour excuse to give up. Complaining is denying our cross instead of denying ourselves. We operate in an immature nature if we continue to complain. We must begin to be thankful in all things, even if we disapprove of or if we are dissatisfied with our reality. Complaining implies that all will not be well unless the change that we want to see occurs immediately. Whenever we complain, we neither give in nor negotiate the outcome we demand; it must be the way we feel it should be.

While continuing my faith journey, I recall that I had a neighbor who was also a single parent struggling to pay bills and raise a child alone. Her methods were to sleep with a guy and have him pay her bills. She explained her method and suggested that I try it out with the guy's friend to get my power bill paid. She told me that it was ok, that my child and I would not be in the dark, and that I could continue to get other bills paid by this same method. I listened to her, but I never felt it was for me. I was learning to trust GOD. I did meet the two young men at my neighbor's home. The best way to end this story is to say I heard GOD's voice more clearly and obtained greater revelation than ever by candlelight. I could not go through with someone else's method for my life when GOD had shown me that I could trust in HIM. I also must mention that my neighbor never spoke with me again after I declined to live according to her method. Thank GOD for that.

There is no need to complain. **GOD has given unto us everything that pertains to life and godliness (2 Peter 1:3).** We need to obtain a great relationship with GOD and know for certain that we are well taken care of by Him. The scriptures say **"eyes have not seen nor ears heard, neither have it entered into the hearts of men the things GOD has prepared for those who love Him"** (1 Corinthians 2:9).

We must get to know GOD and love Him for who He is. We will begin to have the mind of Christ and we will begin to understand the characteristics of GOD. We can be transformed into His nature and become gradually more like Him. Because **in Him we live, move and have our being (Acts 17:28).**

The words we speak acquire life from us. Positive words are as powerful as negative words. Words spoken with conviction and belief produce that which has been uttered. If we speak negative words, we will have what we say. If we speak positive words, we will have what we say. But if we speak the Word of GOD, we will have what we say in abundance.

We shall have what we say (Mark 11:22 - 23). If the words are always negative, we produce a negative reaction. We may wonder why nothing seems to work out for us. It is because words were spoken negatively, and now are producing the fruit of that which was spoken. Complaining gives off negative energy.

The negative energy of complaining makes one weak. Sometimes we make negative statements when we do not see our accomplishments as great. Still, there are ways to accomplish success including planning and meeting individual goals; making sure deadlines are completed on time; being active and enjoying everyday life; and dealing with stress and failures with a positive outlook. We must start to convince ourselves to have a grateful heart. How can we show GOD that we are grateful if all we do is complain?

People complain about the weather. The weather will not change just because we are not satisfied with its current state. It is GOD's determination as to what type of weather we will have each day. We must adapt to the weather. It does not have to adapt to us. GOD knows what the earth needs just as He knows what we need. GOD has designed the seasons, and He is aware of the global effects of each element.

GOD's decision to make it rain is His Sovereign decision, and He does not have to confer with the flesh. **It is the Lord's doing and it should be marvelous in our eyes (Mark 12:11).** Instead of complaining about the weather, we should be grateful for being amongst the living. **Every day is the day that the Lord has made and we should rejoice and be glad in it (Psalm 118:24).** GOD has given us another opportunity to glorify Him in the earth. We should be grateful for the privilege to be counted among the living,

We limit the number of complaints that we utter when we view life with a positive outlook. Instead of complaining, we should take the time to express to GOD our deepest gratitude that our present condition is as well as it is. If we look around the world, we could find a minimum of at least two hundred people who would love to trade places with us.

When we are grateful, we begin to grow and to have humility and to realize that our present state could be worse. That is enough for us to be grateful for the remainder of the year. When we are grateful, we gain strength to manage situations that are not so pleasant.

To obtain strength, we must remain positive. If we wish to succeed in life, we need an enormous amount of positive energy flowing from us. If we complain frequently, we display an inability to shoulder the responsibility of being grateful, the responsibility to be humble, and the responsibility to demonstrate the goodness of GOD. Therefore, if we shoulder our responsibility, then we will not always find reasons to complain by blaming something or someone for our inability to believe GOD.

Complaining is accompanied by anger. There is an overwhelming feeling of injustice. When we complain, we make a statement that something happened and it was unfair. We utter words that suggest that we are not mature and display a childlike behavior that says we want things to go as we feel they should.

When we complain we are not looking at our own faults or misdeeds. We are focusing so intensely on the faults of others or the favor of others that we don't see how a change in us can lead to a greater outcome. We can change our attitude if we only decide to be grateful and rest in the fact that **this too shall pass.**

We begin to complain when our passion for life decreases sometimes causing us to no longer desire to live. Complaining makes us miserable and depressed. It will cause stress and a bad disposition. If we complain all the time, we will fail to see the good when it happens. Nothing will seem pleasant and there will always be criticism which causes a spirit of doubt. *If we complain all the time, we are showing evidence of failure and defeat in our lives. We begin to murmur and find fault which results in negative words of defeat and death.*

Instead of complaining we should be like Job and confess **"Naked came I out of my mother's womb, and naked shall I return thither: the Lord gave, and the Lord hath taken away; blessed be the name of the Lord" (Job 1:21).** Despite all the problems we may face in life, we still have the victory in Christ Jesus. We did not bring anything in this world, but GOD has entrusted us with so much. He has trusted us with a vessel that houses something that He loves dearly -- **our souls.** We should feel honored that GOD trusts us with something He highly regards. GOD decided to trust us even before we knew Him, and He made provisions for us all.

Don't Compete, Don't Compare, Don't Complain: Confess!

When we complain, we are suggesting that GOD does not have the right to do whatever He wants whenever He wants. Whenever we meet trouble, we begin to immediately doubt GOD. If we remember all the times when GOD has rescued us, we would not complain when challenging times come.

Struggles and tough times are not to defeat us but to make us strong. GOD knows the end from the beginning. GOD is the one who designed us and placed us on earth. We should know that GOD has our best interest at heart. When we cannot figure out what is next on the agenda of life, we need to have faith in Almighty GOD who has never caused us to go wrong.

I worked for a manufacturing company with a rotating shift schedule. I knew that when I applied for the job. I really liked the job, but the rotating shift was difficult for several reasons. It was hard to schedule things. It created challenges raising a child. It was tough for the body to get used to working the twelve hours days and then switching to working two weeks of twelve hours nights. It was problematic to find a babysitter. My coworkers experienced similar difficulties. We discussed how we liked the job. The pay was decent, but the rotating shift was a bit much for a lot of us. We didn't complain, but we decided to attempt to get the company to consider changing from a two-week rotating schedule to a monthly rotating schedule or alternatively giving us permanent shifts. I wrote the petition and was able to get the whole company to sign it. I delivered the cause and the proposal to all management. I wrote it as if I was an attorney. This was a serious situation and it demanded that management take it seriously. What happened next? I was fired. Wow! And I was denied unemployment by the company. I appealed my unemployment and won. I received checks in the mail. Before I could cash one check, I received another one. Here is the moral of the story: I did not complain, but I put into action the thing I wanted to see changed. I did not worry about losing the job because no change in the rotation would force me to look for employment elsewhere anyway. I never anticipated the firing or winning the unemployment case. The lesson I learned was to never complain, but to take action for change. Always know that there are other options, and do not worry about the drama or the outcome. GOD is our source. I never think of losing while winning is still an option.

Complainers are worriers. Worrying is not faith, and **anything that is not faith is sin.** When we spend our time with sad dispositions, we are not full of the understanding that **"This is the day which the Lord hath made; we will rejoice and be glad in it" (Psalms 118:24)**. The psalmist is confessing joy. The psalmist knows that he did not make the day and that whatever the day will bring will not kill his praise. The day is an enjoyable day despite our situations or circumstances. The day may not be great for all but it is great for someone; therefore, it is a wonderful day. Those of us who complain are not walking in confessions of joy. Complainers are walking in confessions of bitterness and defeat.

There are times circumstances lead to dissatisfaction in our lives. It is our own fault that we end up in situations that cause us to feel defeated. **"But every man is tempted when he is drawn away of his own lust" (James 1:14)**. When we desire to please the flesh more than we desire to please GOD, we will be led to sin. **"Then when lust hath conceived, it bringeth forth sin: and sin, when it is finished, bringeth forth death" (James 1:15)**. We must be aware that complaining about life does not make it better. If we trust GOD at His word, we will confess that **"all is well"** like the Shunammite woman. She confessed it is well to a situation of death and the situation was reversed **(2 Kings 4)**.

GOD even tells us to **speak to the mountain and do not doubt and we shall have whatsoever we say (Mark 11-23)**. If we only realize the situations we are placing in our lives when we complain, then we would begin to make words of confessions because the words we speak make the difference in whether we succeed or fail in life.

Thank YOU, Heavenly Father. We adore YOU for being the one and only true GOD who loves us despite our complaining. Thank YOU for allowing us the opportunity to speak and believe by faith that if we confess instead of complaining, we can see the situation reversed. Thank YOU for the power of the Holy Ghost that dwells within us and helps us to trust YOU more. We bind the spirit of complaint and we release the spirit of confession. We thank YOU in advance for bringing all things to pass. In Jesus' name, Amen.

Success or Failure

Have you ever wondered why some people progress in life much more rapidly than others? Is it because they are destined to be great while others are cursed to be inferior? Not so. There are reasons why people succeed and others do not. Some people plan, and others do not. Some people have confidence, and others do not. Some people are driven, and other people are not.

Success is a concept that can be understood in various ways. Its definition can be highly subjective, varying from person to person. Success often represents the achievement of goals, objectives, or desired outcomes. What those goals and outcomes are can differ depending on individual values, aspirations, and circumstances.

According to Marc Fey, Life Coach for Life Ascent, there are multiple reasons why success is within our reach:

- a new goal tied to a deeply held value or belief
- a key alliance or alliances
- integrity challenges
- psychological barriers
- building a strong personal foundation
- designing and establishing supportive environments
- increasing our capacity

- a positive attitude and mental outlook
- understanding and taking care of our personal energy levels

Success is planning to win. We need to be sure that we connect our goals for success. If we do not plan to win, then we are ultimately waiting to fail. If we do not progress in obtaining a life that is meaningful and productive, then failure is inevitable. Success is a mixture of failures. It is the result of not giving up in difficult times. Success comes from a spirit of determination. Failure comes from a spirit of procrastination.

Failure is the lack of success or the inability to achieve a desired outcome or goal. It is a part of life that everyone experiences at some point. It can take various forms and be interpreted differently depending on the context and individual perspective.

Success is a highly personal and individualized concept. What one person considers a successful life may not align with another person's definition. Also, how one views success can change over time as personal priorities, values, and circumstances change. People equate success with the accomplishment of specific goals or targets they have set for themselves. These goals can be related to various aspects of life, including career, education, personal relationships, health, or personal development.

Failure does not necessarily define a person's overall potential or capabilities. It is often a temporary setback or a specific event that does not reflect a person's worth or abilities. Failure can build resilience and adaptability to changing circumstances. Overcoming failure can be a source of personal strength and growth.

Motivational author of the 20th century Napoleon Hill suggests many causes of failure:

- unfavorable hereditary background
- lack of a well-defined purpose
- lack of ambition to aim above mediocrities
- insufficient education
- lack of self-discipline
- ill health
- unfavorable environment in childhood
- procrastination (waiting for the right time)
- lack of persistence (good starter, poor finisher)

- negative personality
- lack of control of sexual urge
- uncontrollable desire for something for nothing (gambling)
- lack of a well-defined power of decision making (indecisiveness)

Success is the ability to overcome significant challenges, adversity, or obstacles. It represents resilience and the ability to adapt and thrive in the face of difficulties.

Success and failure are major parts of our journey of life. There are circumstances and situations that can cause this journey to be much harder for others. There are no how-to books that completely detail how to start or finish our journeys. There are no detailed hit-or-miss targets that propel individuals to distinct levels in life. There are only experiences that all must encounter. No two journeys are the same. There are similarities in life journeys but different contents. Each has a beginning, and each has an end. Our journey in life is a process that must be completed.

Even before we are born, we must go through life stages. Conception has various stages, and all the stages must be completed before labor and delivery. Nine months of development must be accomplished. There are times pre-maturity can be healthy with treatment and other times pre-maturity can be deformative. The first stage is being a baby followed by being a toddler. Then life progresses from youth to adolescences on to adulthood.

We cannot skip these stages. In each stage, there are certain responsibilities that help to develop and promote progression. While progressing through each stage, an individual must learn traits that enable development. When all stages have been accomplished, we will have characteristics gleaned from our experiences.

The journey is on-going. As an adult, the journey continues and begins to intensify as developmental stages are being put into action by the challenges we face and decisions that we make. Each must walk out the journey. Journeys are difficult, and journeys are easy. Journeys are long and hard. Some journeys are dangerous, adventurous, mysterious, and nonproductive while others are inspiring. Other journeys are courageous and fearful. Journeys are healthy, strong, and talented while others are weak and full of infirmity. Journeys are obedient, and journeys are rebellious. In all our journeys, we experience highs and lows. We experience times when misdeeds go unpunished while others experience times that we are chastened immediately.

To have success in life's experiences, there are things that we must understand. Each journey requires personal responsibilities. We must not compare ourselves with others. We must not compete with one another. We must not complain about mistakes or heartaches along the way. We must have positive confessions.

Failure is not the end of the road but rather a part of the journey toward success and personal growth. How one responds to failure, whether by learning from it, adapting, and persevering, can determine future achievements. Many successful individuals have faced multiple failures on their paths to success and used those experiences to propel themselves forward. Accepting failure as a natural and constructive aspect of life can lead to resilience, self-discovery, and elevated success.

No two journeys are completely alike; therefore, comparison would be insufficient to fairly assess an individual's success or failure. There are too many differences and character traits to compare each equally. Hence, we must not compete or complain about measures of superiority or inferiority due to individual success or failure. And we must be careful of the words that we speak.

Complaining should not be part of our lifestyle. We must be grateful and not regretful. Sometimes it is the sad things that happen to us that make us stronger. Instead of competing, comparing, or complaining, we should confess. We should confess gratitude. We should confess positive affirmations and positive declarations. We should confess life and the wonderful things we can obtain from it.

Also, if we are to obtain a successful life, we must be able to speak with confidence about those things that we believe about ourselves. We must speak positive words that encourage and uplift not just ourselves but also our children, our government, our neighbors, our families, our communities, and the nations. We must confess what will happen in our lives. Confessions of positive expectations can produce greater outcomes. If we devote more time to positive confessions instead of complaints, success will be attained.

It is important to understand that to become successful we must have positive confessions all the time. The words spoken produce a harvest.

Negative words produce a negative harvest, and positive words produce a positive harvest. All the things that we speak produce fruits just like the things that we think in our hearts reflect our speech. Also, the words we speak become life. To be successful, there must be a cheerful outlook flowing from within us. We learn that **whatever state we are in, we should strive to be content.**

Father, give us the wisdom to speak words of positive confession. Help us to be more appreciative about the life we have so that we can be more grateful and not complain. Lord, help us to value the goodness in others so that we will not compete but let us desire to learn from one another. Father, help us to not compare ourselves with others to be resentful or jealous of the goodness that YOU bestow on those around us, but let us look closer at our own lives and value the goodness that YOU have given us. In Jesus' name, we pray. Amen.

Contentment

Contentment is a satisfaction with our present state of being. It is a pleasure and a peace that permeates the current circumstances. It is a relaxed attitude to trust GOD despite present economic, emotional, or personal situations. Contentment is a calmness to accept the life that GOD has planned. It is a declaration that the goodness of GOD is great, and there is no need to be weary.

The earliest references to the state of contentment are found in the reference to the middah (personal attribute) of Samayach B'Chelko. The expression comes from the word samayach (root Sin-Mem-Chet) meaning "happiness, joy or contentment" and chelko (root Chet-Lamed-Kuf) meaning "portion, lot, or piece" and combined mean contentment with one's lot in life. The attribute is referred to in the Mishnahic source which says Ben Zoma said: "Who is rich -- those who are happy with their portion."

Contentment is not settling; it is not a position of never reaching higher levels. It is with these things in mind that the present well-being is enough for the right now **(Philippians 4:11).** It is a satisfied heart that does not desire to scheme or go through extreme measures to achieve merits illegitimately. Contentment is obtained by accepting oneself. No matter how difficult or how challenging life may be, it is a security in finding peace within.

I found peace in living without power instead of subjecting myself to something I would later regret. I faced head on the thing that would be uncomfortable, and in doing so found a greater sense of accomplishment and strength. I was intentional about getting through my circumstances without yielding to temptations or strategies of the enemy. I found an inner peace to be content and know that things were not always going to be like this.

Peace is the reward for accepting that life is well, and it is bearable. There is also confidence in accepting well enough as a temporary state and a hope that things will change. Once we have confidence and hope, we can be content about life's difficulties.

Sometimes the status of life may be long and weary, but with contentment there is always hope. There is always an assurance that everything will work out. If we continue to trust and have faith in GOD, we can live our lives with contentment; we won't worry about gaining the world's wealth because GOD is the supplier of all things **(1 Timothy 6:6 and 1 Timothy 6:8).**

Contentment does not exclude ambition, personal growth, or the pursuit of goals. It is contentment that allows individuals to pursue their goals from a place of inner peace and balance rather than from a sense of desperation or emptiness.

I heard the Lord saying finish what you started. GOD blessed me with a career before I finished school. I often refer to it as putting the horse before the cart. I got hired with the phone company, and I have been there for more than 23 years now. I heard the voice speak so clearly. *Finish what you started.* I had dropped out of college to take care of my daughter. I had often thought about going back and finishing, but I never was intentional about it. But I knew that was the message that I received. So, I went back and got my degree in Computer Science. It was a tremendous victory. Thank you, Lord! I know that GOD was with me. I was there and enjoyed the journey, but it was difficult. Thank GOD I had developed faith before going back to college. I was asking the HOLY SPIRIT to teach me calculus and physics. Whew! Thanks be to GOD who knows all things. In my studies, I gained more faith in GOD.

If we have faith in GOD and **believe that He will supply all our needs,** then there is no need for complaining. **GOD knows what we need, and He has promised to help us and never leave us (Hebrews 13:5).**

Contentment also comes from faith. It is faith that gives the assurance that things will always improve. It is also the faith that comforts the heart to realize that situations could have been worse. Therefore, contentment is a way of being grateful for those things we do have. We know that things can be more dreadful than they are, so we must be patient. We also must be grateful and give thanks that our situations are not tragic. Gratitude is the power to make contentment a peaceful decision, and it will give us the wisdom to not complain.

When we complain, we suggest that we know what is best for our lives. We do not expect to suffer at all. We complain if it rains, and we complain if the sun shines. We are constantly complaining about life situations but never take any necessary steps for change. **Jesus** told His disciples to **pick up their crosses and follow Him**. The cross is symbolic of troubles and indicates that we all will face trouble at times, but we must pick up those things that trouble us and continue to follow Jesus.

Picking up our crosses is metaphoric for carrying our burdens instead of letting our burdens carry us. We need to face our circumstances and continue to follow Christ. We are victorious because we understand that we win if we follow the guidelines of our Creator. We face inconvenient situations in life, and they will never win over us. The Word of GOD states that **there are MANY afflictions of the righteous, but the Lord delivers us from them all (Psalms 34).**

Complaining comes about because of a lack of contentment. We are never satisfied. We are never at peace with our present circumstances. We are unable to see the brighter side of things. We never conclude difficulties with a cheerful outlook. We confess negativity in our lives and wonder why things never change for us.

We also compare the past with the present. We speak about how life used to be. We speak about how we wish things were the same as they used to be. We do not realize how great and wonderful things can be for us right now if we were content.

When we are content, we are saying to GOD I trust YOU. We are happy with the value of life instead of making material things valuable.

In late 2011, I received a promotion that required me to relocate to Denver, Colorado. It was an abrupt transition; I didn't have time to sell my home. I inquired about renting and had a friend with a family member in need of a stable place to stay. I had no idea how long I would be in Denver. Following my friend's advice, I drew up the rental arrangement. I immediately called on family members to go to my home and get whatever items that they wanted or needed so that my home was ready to lease.

I was very vulnerable because I was fourteen hundred miles away from my home. I allowed my family to enter as much as necessary to remove all furniture and other items to get the home ready for the tenant's two month move in date. I mentioned my earlier struggles in life. But now I was content. For eleven years, I was stable. I had a great job, finished school, and purchased my home.

I left for Denver, but the remarkable part of this story is that I learned to release. I let go of all the material things that I thought were so dear to me. I had so many things that I obtained – items that years ago I had believed were out of reach. I am a towel fanatic. I had so many bath towels that I had recently purchased. So many! It's funny when I think on it now. The towels were one of the hardest items to let go of, along with my books and shoes. But a peace and contentment fell on me. I learned the power of release. I didn't rent the home. The person backed out on the day to sign the lease. Today, all the things that I released I have gotten back and much more. Thank GOD for the lesson, because it has taught me to be content no matter if I am up or down. I feel like the New Testament writer Paul in that whatever state I find myself I realize that I am content. It has made me trust GOD more. The more I walk closer to HIM the more I realize nothing is greater than HIS blessings for me.

If we walk closer to GOD, we will begin to see just how unimportant material things are. We will cease to complain about the weather or the economic situations in the world. **We will have perfect peace because our mind is stayed on GOD.**

Content is another word for grateful. We are grateful that GOD has changed our present conditions. We are grateful and count it indeed an honor and a privilege to call upon His name. Before we ask GOD for anything, we need to be content with what He has already done. We need to be content because we did not wake up on the pavement, and we also need to be content if we did. We need to be content because GOD preserves the sanity of our minds. We need to be content that we are not lying in a hospital bed or that we must pay for medical services. We need to be content for our emotional well-being. We need to be content to have food, clothes, and shelter. We need to be content that GOD is merciful and loves us all no matter what we have done. With contentment we can build a strong resolve to be determined to overcome all obstacles we face.

Father, show us how to be content because with godliness there is great gain. Help us to learn to be content no matter what our present circumstance appears to be. YOU are a very present help in times of trouble. Let us know that YOU will supply all our needs according to YOUR riches in Glory and that YOU perfect those things that concern us. YOU will never leave us nor forsake us. We must learn to count it all joy, and let patience have her perfect work. Because of the spirit of contentment, we will praise YOU even more. In Jesus' name, Amen.

Determination

The quality of mind which reaches definite conclusions is one of the ways **Webster** defines determination. We must reach a conclusion to never look back and be determined to see the end. Paul stresses in **Philippians 3** that his conclusion is to **follow that which has apprehended or taken hold onto him**. He can neither shake it nor deny it, but he plans to keep going forward to obtain it. He does not try to explain the reasoning for moving forward, but later goes on to say that GOD will reveal it.

To gain this type of mindset we must realize that whatever was done in the past will not halt our future so we must press forward. We must understand that past mistakes and present situations do not forfeit future promises. Let me say that again. Our past mistakes and present situations DO NOT forfeit future promises. If GOD promised, then He is more than capable to perform it.

Determination is a mental and emotional quality characterized by a strong, unwavering commitment to achieving a goal despite obstacles, difficulties, setbacks, or challenges. It involves having a firm resolve and the willpower to persist and stay focused on one's objectives, even when faced with adversity or the desire to give up. Determination is a key factor in achieving success and overcoming obstacles.

For determination to manifest, there must be a tremendous amount of faith applied. Faith is needed to counterattack the doubts and the fears that blind the vision and choke the purpose. The faith that we have must be a three-fold objective. It is a faith that says **all things are possible to those who believe (Mark 9:23), and with GOD, all things are possible (Matthew 19:26)**. Determination involves a high level of persistence and the willingness to keep going, even when faced with setbacks or obstacles. It requires the ability to bounce back from failures and disappointments.

I moved to the Atlanta metro area back in the late 1980s. Circumstances and situations caused me to move back to my hometown of Bibb County. I knew that my setback was not a stay back. I was able to move back to the Atlanta metro area about a year later. I confessed that I was never moving back to Bibb County. I was determined that if I could not make it to the Atlanta metro area I would move to Tennessee. I did not want to keep moving back to the small town of Macon, Georgia where there were limited opportunities. I was determined I would never live there again. I confessed it, I believed it, and I have no desire to return.

There is a faith of confession we must speak. We must speak words of life and not of death. We can say the wrong things. We must be determined and not speak about past mistakes. Instead, we must say that we will walk in destiny. Our eyes are focused, our feet are moving, and we pray that GOD will **give us a plain path into His presence**.

Determination often goes hand-in-hand with resilience. It involves the ability to withstand adversity, criticism, or challenges without losing sight of the goal.

We do not need to try and map out the steps because the course has been set from Eden to Eternity. There is no need to deviate because the Master has set the original courses for all our lives. "**He knows the plans that He has towards us to prosper us, to give us a hope and a future**" **(Jeremiah 29:11).**

To be determined means to never give up no matter the pace, no matter the race, no matter the opposition. To see the end results, we must complete the race. To obtain the goal, we must finish the task. If we give up, the only thing that we will have procured is regret.

We cannot live our lives looking back and holding onto regret. We are challenged because if something is worth having, it is worth working hard to acquire. If we always take the effortless way out, we will never know the road to lead others.

Giving in and giving up are the easiest things to do. It takes no effort to accomplish either. There are no actions or tasks. Standing still is stagnant behavior. It will result in zero accountability and zero attainability. Determination takes a superpower called tenacity. It is the willingness to proceed intentionally into achievement. To complete a goal is to experience great victory and great joy.

Blindly facing obstacles to win is an unexplainable methodology. It is like walking into a dark room looking for a needle. You have no point of contact and it seems futile, but you feel you must continue the search. Your faith tells you something will happen, and you will find what you are looking for. Doubt tells you do not be led into useless actions that will only have you feeling defeated. That is when determination rushes into your mind and soothes the matter. Determination reminds you of why you started and the reason you must continue.

While determination involves persistence, it also requires adaptability. Sometimes, individuals need to adjust their strategies or approach when facing unexpected challenges. Having a support system, such as friends, family, mentors, or a community, can provide encouragement and motivation to stay determined.

Determination can be applied to various aspects of life, including personal goals, academic pursuits, career objectives, athletics, creative endeavors, and more. It is a valuable quality that can help individuals overcome obstacles and achieve success, even in the face of significant challenges or adversity.

If we begin to confess what we want to see manifested in our lives, we will be determined to see it. We will be determined to believe that we will receive it. We will develop the type of faith that will not waver and be ready to receive in due season.

We make a conscious decision everyday about what we will do. We will wake up, wash our face, brush our teeth, comb our hair, and go to school or work. We can also make a conscious decision to be determined to see our dreams and our aspirations to the end. We can be determined that we will believe GOD no matter how terrible things look.

One of the things we must determine to do is be effective in our everyday life. We must make our lives live on after we are gone. We do that by positively affecting someone else's life. To be determined, we must have the power to no longer depend on our senses. We must begin to operate in the supernatural to obtain those things that are sometimes out of our reach. Jesus told His disciples **"Behold I give you power."**

Being determined and confessing our future is a bold step. It takes courage to be determined. In **Psalms 27,** the writer stresses to **"be of a good courage and GOD will strengthen our hearts."** We need strong hearts to be determined. We must have a heart that endures the trials and the stresses of everyday life. A heart that depends on and trusts GOD no matter what the senses are suggesting. A heart that is willing to change during the test and not after the test.

A change means to begin again. To be determined means to never stop going. We may have to change the way we are going, but never change the why we are going. To reach a definite conclusion, we need determination to be strong-minded, single-minded, and unwavering. We may be referred to as stubborn-minded, but we must be resilient and not be moved.

Paul was determined he would preach the gospel no matter what situations he faced. He decided that he would preach from a jail cell. He would praise GOD even though he was in chains. He would continue to live his life and be determined to serve GOD. He was determined to be a prisoner for Christ. We need the same attitude that our brother Paul had even when he was facing death. He said, **"none of these things move me" (Acts 20:24).**

Determination is a drive; it is a never-ending force that directs us to the goals in mind. It is a continuation of hope and victory. It is the essence of a reality that was once a thought or a dream but now is evident.

Determination supersedes a desire; it runs along with our journey, and it overtakes the fear to procrastinate or fail. We must be determined to win if it looks like everyone before us has failed. We must be determined to fight even if the battle looks like it cannot be won. We must be determined not to hear words that are negative and cause us to doubt or fear. We must be determined to speak life to situations, and we must be determined to begin to confess positive words in our everyday challenges. We must be determined to not accept losing while winning is still an option.

We must be determined to **hunger and thirst for righteousness** -- to be filled not just with natural food, but with spiritual food as well. We must confess that we have our eyes opened so that we may see and our ears opened so that we may hear. Determination is not just practical. It is spiritual because determination opposes generalization.

Sometimes it is not a popular thing to be determined. It can have negative effects. People we love may turn against us because they cannot see our vision. They may try to convince us to give up and try something new. When we have a made-up mind, there is nothing that can stop our determination.

Father, help us to hold fast to our confessions and be determined to trust YOU at any cost. Help us to be determined to live a life that pleases YOU. Father, we know determination takes grit and the ability to stand and withstand. Father, give us wisdom in every area where we lack. Give us the fortitude to be determined to finish the race no matter the cost because we trust YOU. In Jesus' name, Amen.

Joy

Joy is indescribable; it is a reaction that confuses emotions. Joy is expressed with laughter and great glee. At other times, it is expressed with tears. Whenever we see someone crying, we immediately attribute the tears to sadness, but there are times when we are overwhelmed with joy and we cry. It is a feeling that takes control of our ability to rationalize an emotional process. When we experience extraordinary joy, we tend to inexplicably react by laughing and crying at the same time.

Joy is one of the nine divine ingredients that make up the fruit given by the Holy Spirit. It is a mixture that sits in the middle of love and peace. The first three that if obtained will help with the next six divine ingredients. We cannot have joy without love and peace. If we love one another (one of the great commandments), then we will have joy. If we have peace, we have pleasure with GOD. Therefore, we are not consumed with the issues of life. We are stable, and we don't let circumstances overtake us. **But the fruit of the Spirit is love, joy, peace, longsuffering, gentleness, goodness, faith, meekness, temperance: against such there is no law (Galatians 5:22 - 23).**

Our brother James says **to count it all** joy when we meet up with diverse types of temptations. If we know that temptations are putting our faith on trial, then patience will step in and work for us. If we **let patience have her perfect work,** meaning that we do not try to work out our problems ourselves, we remain confident and see the situation all the way to completion. Afterwards, we will be mature and lack nothing, thereby causing us to demonstrate joy. **My brethren, count it all joy when ye fall into divers' temptations; knowing this, that the trying of your faith worketh patience. But let patience have her perfect work, that ye may be perfect and entire, wanting nothing (James 1:2-4).**

The dictionary describes joy as **an emotion caused by events or happenings. It is an expression not only of great delight but of great inner peace**. To experience joy there must be a divine origin of a peaceful life. There are those of us who experience joy after obtaining goals, winning championships, or seeing a loved one after an extended period. These are all achieved through human efforts and cannot be compared with the divine element of the joy that is mentioned earlier. Devine joy is inexpressible because it comes with a mixture of hope, love, faith, peace, meekness, gentleness, kindness, self-control, and patience all combined in an undetermined amount. Human words can never sufficiently describe that which the Holy Spirit gives.

I experienced a joy that cannot be explained when I won my unemployment case against the company that fired me. I was so overjoyed that I cried. I stood up against a big company. With the help of GOD, I won. I cannot describe the emotions that swept over me when I was granted all my benefits. I felt relieved that the case was over. I felt courageous. I felt victorious. I felt so many things at once. I could not articulate the joy that I felt. It was unspeakable, unexplainable, unreal.

Matthew Henry, an English theologian of the seventeenth century, describes joy **as a constant delight in GOD and a cheerful conversation with one another**. Joy is offered to us as a reward for our acceptance of the Holy Spirit. It is not contingent on works of our flesh. It is a recommended source for daily spiritual growth. Joy is requested in times of heaviness of heart. Joy is a heart-lifting and warm feeling for which there is no logical reason other than a divine measure of response that we must delight in GOD.

Joy provides an assurance to us while we endure the troubles that we face. Joy is not dismissed from us. Once it is presented it is for keeps. It is full. **Hitherto have ye asked nothing in my name: ask, and ye shall receive, that your joy may be full (John 16:24).**

Thou wilt shew me the path of life: in thy presence is fulness of joy; at thy right hand there are pleasures for evermore **(Psalms 16:11)**. Joy is often expressed outwardly through smiles, laughter, dancing, and other forms of exuberance. It is a contagious emotion that can be shared and spread to others.

If we have joy, we do not have a need to compete, compare or complain. Whenever we witness someone achieving a goal or experiencing an event of a lifetime, we display joy too. Because of the love that we have, we will rejoice with them as though it was our own achievement even though we do not reap any benefits. Because of the peace that we have in our lives, we can share their glad tidings. Joy does not allow us to feel competitive towards them or feel inferior so that we must complain about their good fortune. We rejoice because we have a constant delight in GOD, knowing that if He does remarkable things for them He will do remarkable things for us.

Joy is connected to the appreciation of life's blessings, both big and small. It can develop from gratitude for the people, experiences, and instances that bring happiness. Joy is a complex emotion that can vary from person to person and from one situation to another. What brings joy to one person may not necessarily have the same effect on another. Joy can coexist with other emotions. People may experience a range of emotions in their lives including moments of joy during challenges and difficulties.

Having joy can eliminate the need to worry or complain. Joy keeps our hearts in a state of gratitude. We can feel satisfaction, a fullness and a rewarding sense of pride that comes from knowing that life has its moments of balance. Joy is the practice of mindfulness, gratitude, engaging in activities that bring happiness, and focusing on positive aspects of life. Joy is a valuable and enriching emotion that contributes to an overall sense of fulfillment.

Joy is the opposite of sadness. We have all felt some type of sadness and experienced the hopelessness that can accompany it. Sadness causes us to complain. We complain when we feel defeated and mistreated. We complain when we feel a loss. Sadness is a normal emotion but it is not an emotion we should remain in for long periods of time. There must be a point when we normalize our emotions to break out of sadness. If we remain in a state of sadness for too long, it will become our disposition. We have many more positive things in our lives than we do negative. We must focus on the good to balance our emotions. Nothing lasts forever, and there is always a brighter day. We cannot keep complaining as though we have never had greater times. There are storms, and the impact of those storms can be detrimental to human lives, but the purpose of those storms is meant to bring about some sort of balance to the environment. **"Hurricanes may also provide ecological benefits to tropical and sub-tropical environments. Rainfall gives a boost to wetlands and flushes out lagoons, removing waste and weeds. Hurricane winds and waves move sediment from bays into marsh areas, revitalizing nutrient supplies"** (www.huricanescience.org).

We as humans may never understand, but GOD is all wise. We must trust Him with all aspects of the divine and the natural course of things. The more we trust and rely on GOD, the more our joy is fulfilled. We have the blessed assurance that **all things are working for our good**. Joy should be a natural and spiritual response to keep us from complaining in tough times.

Father, thank YOU for YOUR Holy Spirit that gives us the fruit; may we partake of all that is freely given to us. Thank YOU for the joy that will never be taken from us. Help us to always display it, regardless of our situations or our circumstances. Let us always be aware of YOUR goodness towards us so that we can continue to be full of joy. We thank YOU for a plain path that will lead us into YOUR presence and there we will obtain fullness of joy and pleasures evermore. In Jesus' name we pray, Amen.

Character

Imagine we are all genies, and we can instantly initiate change just by the words we speak. Would we be better or worse in our relationships? Would we have positive or negative motives in dealing with the cares of this life? What if the words that we spoke manifested as soon as we released them from our lips? Would we be selective in choosing our words? What if we could change instances of our lives by going home each night and rewinding a video tape of our daily activities? Would it persuade us to make better decisions the next day to improve our character?

Frank Damazio in his book *The Making of a Leader* defines character as "the seat of one's moral being; the inner life of man; it will reflect either the traits of the sinful nature (being influenced by the world) or the traits of the divine nature (being influenced by the Word of GOD)." He also states that, "character is the combination of qualities distinguishing any person or class of persons." He finally states that "Character is the sum total of all positive and negative qualities in our lives, exemplified by one's thoughts, values, motivations, attitudes, feelings, and actions."

The character we display is a response from our motives, actions, reactions, and even the words that we speak. We live our lives based on choices that originate from our character. We choose to get up or stay in bed. We choose to eat or not eat breakfast. We choose to go to work or stay at home. Our lives are a direct reflection of the choices we make, and those choices can lead to positive as well as negative reactions.

We all face conflicts, and it is common. But we also have a high priest who knows and understands what we go through. We wish we could avoid all conflict. We all have experienced conflicts that we wished we had never encountered. And we certainly wish we would have no more.

Character refers to the moral and ethical qualities, values, traits, and principles that define an individual's identity and guide their behavior. It is the quality of a person's personality that shapes how they interact with others and make decisions. Character is often seen as a reflection of one's integrity, honesty, and moral compass.

Our character is shaped not by the trouble we encounter but by how we respond to the trouble. Character is also formed by the way we manage trouble that produces an outcome for successful living. If we live our lives comparing, competing, or complaining, we will have negative characteristics. But if we live our lives confessing positive declarations, we live victoriously.

Character involves so much of us it is hard to narrow it all down. Character is respect for oneself and others. It is a positive reflection of good character. It involves treating others with courtesy, empathy, and consideration, regardless of differences in background, beliefs, or opinions. Character is honesty. Being honest is a key element of a positive character. It requires truthfulness, transparency, and a commitment to moral communication. Our thoughts, our speech, our actions all determine our character.

Our character is reflective in everything we do. When we display attitudes of anger or any type of negative actions, it describes our character. When we live our lives believing GOD and confessing His words, our character is full of faith. We can change our character by making decisions to change our attitude and our thought life which will enable us to be more positive and operate on godly principles.

I remember when my character was full of flaws, but my desire to please GOD made me want to change my attitude to correct my character. I wanted to obey GOD and love others. I had to start being conscious of the words that I spoke. I had to change the way that I thought about people in general to learn to love others. I was not always kind or considerate to others. I had my space, and I did not want anyone to invade it. I was not deliberately impolite, but I was easily provoked. I used the fact that I did not disrupt others to justify my behavior when others were disrespectful to me. I intentionally used the reason that I was provoked as a means of retribution for old and new. The anger that I displayed was targeted at those who may or may not have caused the trauma to be reignited. My attitude suggested that my reactions were justifiable. But when the HOLY SPIRIT became my helper and my comforter, I was convicted. I was not letting GOD fight for me. I had to release my pride and realize that whenever something happens to me without me causing it to happen, it is GOD getting me in trouble. And if GOD gets me in trouble, then GOD will get me out of trouble. Peter was asleep when the angel came to break him out of prison. GOD has a strategy that wins every time. I learned to let GOD have His way in all circumstances of my life. This is not easy to accomplish all the time. I had to start confessing what I wanted to see in my life.

Positive confessions are just as easy to make as negative confessions. If we cannot think of anything positive to confess on our own, we can always confess what GOD says. **"We are redeemed, we are more than conquers and we have the victory in Christ Jesus. We are mighty through GOD. We have power that is over all the power of the enemy."**

In all these confessions, it did not require anything from us for these confessions to become truth. So, all we must do is believe each one of these confessions and our character will reflect what each of these confessions declares. If we decide not to adjust our attitudes to reflect positive behavior, then we experience character flaws.

Father, create in us a clean heart and the right spirit. Teach us YOUR ways and give us the ability to direct our lives in the way that YOU have ordained us to go. Order our steps in YOUR word and let no iniquity have dominion over us. Give us the tongue of the learned that we would speak words of faith and confess that which YOU have spoken. Father, help us to change the things about us that causes us to be in opposition to what YOU have created us to be. In Jesus' name, Amen.

Prayer

P rayer is communication with the **ONE** who can transform circumstances and situations for the greater good. Prayer is displayed in a sigh, a cry, a thought, and even a song. Prayer is the opportunity of expression. It is an invitation by the one making the petition, and it is complimented with thanksgiving. There are different types of prayers. There are prayers of a repented soul. There are prayers of thanksgiving, prayers of intercessions, and prayers of praise and adoration. Prayer is a commitment to trust that only GOD can supply every need. It is a deep trust for change.

Prayer is often not taught because it is a conversation. There are methods that can help improve prayer, but no one can instruct anyone on the way to communicate with GOD. I remember when I joined the adult softball team. I befriended an older adult. She was about five or six years older than me. I was seventeen and a high school senior. After the softball season ended, I started hanging out with my friend Kwajelyn. She and I would go to a lot of different places together. We went to parties, clubs, and after-hour joints, and we spent time with friends at different homes. My friend did not work. She was able to go and do whatever without a schedule. I was careful to confess that I would not drop out of high school. GOD had me making positive confessions, and I did not realize it. I will tell this story to reflect on how I learned to pray. After hanging out with my friend, it would be so late that I would spend the night at her place. No matter what time we came in from our events I saw my friend get down on her knees and pray. I did not hear what she said. I just remember that her posture and consistency prompted me to do the same. She never instructed me to follow her nor did she tell me what to say. I am not sure if she knows it, but I am so grateful for her being in my life for this reason. I must admit I had no idea what to say. After I got on my knees, it seemed the words to say came to me naturally. My fellowship with GOD had started. We became great friends, and then I understood what having a father really meant. I developed a lasting and strong prayer life just by having an attitude to try and revere GOD. I approached it with a childlike experience of just wanting to say "Hello GOD, how are you?"

Prayer is an expression of a great need for change. It is a combination of hope and faith working together to determine a greater outcome. Prayer is also a confession. It is a statement that change will come forth. It is a declaration, a decree that will be established.

Prayer is a deep desire to see change occur. Sometimes prayers are answered right away, and sometimes prayer is a process. Prayer is a spiritual act that is executed by natural behavior. Prayer is spiritual because the One who answers is Spiritual. There are always answers to prayer. GOD says call unto me and I will answer. Sometimes we think that our prayers go unanswered, but that would make GOD out to be a liar. There are two immutable things that prevents GOD from lying: His Word and His Promise. He cannot change HIS Word. He can change His methods. He says He will answer. If prayer is spiritual and the One who answers is spiritual, then the answer will be spiritual. The flesh cannot comprehend the things of the spirit; therefore, people suggest that prayers go unanswered. In fact, all prayers have the answers of yes, no or wait. Because GOD is all knowing, He determines the outcome of the answer. If we trust GOD, we will trust that His way is the best way.

Jesus taught His disciples to pray. He gave them the formula for prayer. It is the way in which we should approach our King. He taught them how to adore and exalt the Father. It is how we should honor Him for His goodness towards us and how we should acknowledge that He is our only source. He has already provided all our needs for us each day. **After this manner therefore pray ye: Our Father which art in heaven, Hallowed be thy name. Thy kingdom come; Thy will be done on earth, as it is in heaven. Give us this day our daily bread. And forgive us our debts,** as we forgive our debtors. And lead us not into temptation, but deliver us from evil: For thine is the kingdom, and the power, and the glory, forever. Amen (Matthew 6:9-13).

Admiration

Christ gave us a formula for prayer. In this manner, first we must acknowledge who we are praying to: **Our Father**. The most honorable and prestigious role is that of a Father. GOD is the Father to us all, and we acknowledge the greatest relationship that binds all together. This is to whom we make our confessions, our intercessions, our moans, and our request because **He knows what we have need of before we ask**. This is His responsibility, and He knows all too well what should be provided.

Exaltation

Hallow be His name. Holy is His name. To "**hallow** the name" includes not only the inward attitude and outward action of profound reverence and active praise, but also that personal relationship which causes loving obedience and an aggressive desire to become more like Him. Calling on His name reveals the presence of GOD and His glory.

We now exalt His name. To exalt means to praise, glorify, or honor; heighten or intensify. What we do is lift His name to magnify it. What it does is allow us to tell GOD how great He is in our hearts and in our lives. We lift Him to show that we can see how impressive He is, and it gives us more revelation of who He is. **O LORD our Lord, how excellent is thy name in all the earth! (Psalms 8:9).**

Manifestation

Thirdly, we pray for His righteousness, His peace, and His joy to come. For **His Kingdom to come**. The Kingdom is where the King rules. So, we pray for His Kingdom to come into our hearts, our minds, and our lives. Let His Kingdom rule on our behalf, for He is the King of Glory.

Transformation

Fourthly, we pray for His will to be done on earth. It is the Father's will that all come into the knowledge of who He is for this is life eternal. **"And this is life eternal, that we might know thee the only true GOD, and Jesus Christ, whom thou hast sent" (John 17:3).** It is also His will that none should perish. **"The Lord is not slack concerning his promise, as men count slackness; but is longsuffering to us-ward, not willing that any should perish, but that all should come to repentance" (2 Peter 3:9).**

It is the Father's will to have obedient children, for the transformation of His will on earth **as it is in Heaven**. All obey Him in Heaven, and we should pray for the divine likeness to manifest on earth. Nature obeys, and the beasts obey, but His children do not. We are formed in His likeness but we are to resemble Him. So, for this we must pray.

Revelation

Next, we make our request known to Him. We ask for provisions of the day. **Sufficient today is the evil thereof.** We should only be concerned with the matters of the day. The word declares that we **take no thought of what we should eat or what we should wear. For our Father knows the things of which we have need.** So, the prayer is for His daily bread, a word from the Father that we may get the manna that we need. Give us a Ramah word from on High that will meet us where we are.

We may not all get the same word, but to each of us it will be given as daily provision. Give it to us because it will sustain us. It will encourage us. It will equip us, and it will transform us to make us what He would have us to be.

Reformation

Then, we pray for forgiveness. **Forgive us our debts. We all fall short of Glory.** GOD did not make us perfect for one reason, and that is we would have no need to call on Him. GOD could have put perfection in each one of His creations, but because He is a GOD of love and a Father who desires relationship, we have a need to continually come to Him. He wants 100% dependence on Him. The **Father is faithful and just forgives us** if we confess. He does not stop there. He cleanses us and gives us another chance to get it right. His forgiveness is not for us. The word declares that He **forgives us for His name's sake.** He does not want to go down with a reputation that He is not just, that He is not a righteous judge who shows mercy. So, He forgives. And then He requires the same of His children. We must **forgive our debtors.** Jesus told His disciples to forgive those who wrong us **"seventy times seven that is the number of times we must forgive our brother."** If we expect to get forgiveness, then why not expect to give it?

Restoration

Also, we pray that the Father would **lead us not into temptation.** Because of the humbleness of the child of GOD, the Spirit leads him. So, the prayer is not that we would be persuaded to do what is unpleasing, but that the Spirit would reroute the path that will lead us away from that which is not pleasing. The word declares that **we are led away after our own lust.** But the request is to lead us away from those things that tempt us. The Spirit knows the mind of man. Our spirit agrees with the Holy Spirit. When we pray and ask for help with the things that weaken us or **the sin and the weight that so easily besets us,** the helper is ready to assist and **deliver us from all evil.**

The things we may not be aware of hinder us, but the Father is aware and ready to aid us. There are multiple afflictions of the righteous, but the Lord delivers us from them all. And these are but light afflictions which cannot compare with the Glory that shall be revealed. The sufferings are not to be held up against the Glory; it just does not compare. But after we have suffered awhile, He will perfect us, settle us, and establish us. The Lord knows what we require before we ask.

Magnification

Lastly, we give glory to the Highest. We celebrate HIM. Thine is the Kingdom. **Thine, O LORD, is the greatness, and the power, and the glory, and the victory, and the majesty: for all that is in the heaven and in the earth is thine; thine is the kingdom, O LORD, and thou art exalted as head above all (1 Chronicles 29:11).**

As the prayer ends, we now substantiate why we can request all things with confidence. GOD is more than capable of overseeing the greatest request. We confirm it because this is YOUR **Kingdom.** Therefore, YOU are the King, and we proclaim that we know to whom we have placed such heavy demands. Because we are sure that YOU can **do exceedingly and abundantly above all that we have asked or imagine YOU to do**. And because we rely on YOU to fulfill all these requests, not only are YOU the King but YOU are the **Kingdom**. YOU are the **Power** and the **Glory** behind the throne. YOU reign forever. YOU are the **Dominion,** the supreme authority. YOU rule **forever and ever**. YOUR Kingdom shall never end. Amen. And so, it is.

Prayer is also a learned behavior. It is a high priority that shows how one values a relationship with GOD. It is a tool of strength and a measure of love. It is a communication device that says He is listening, and He is speaking, yet He already answered.

Prayer is obedience to the command to **pray always without ceasing.** It is a recommendation as well as a commandment. It will give confidence to a heart that says in all things I trust GOD and a heart that says I will not attempt to manage that which my Father can do so well. I will not put my hands to it because GOD will manage a greater outcome for me. When the power of prayer is obtained, it is only maintained by the persistence and constant desire to continue therein.

Prayer is a tool that if used each day will help to control strong desires to compete, complain or compare. It will help to make a strong confession happen. If prayer is utilized, it will equip one with everything needed to be successful in both the spiritual and the natural realms.

Praying for others will keep us from competing with one another. Whenever we **esteem others higher than ourselves,** we say that we want to see them blessed. We want them to receive what GOD has for them. We want to see them walking in prosperity. We want to see their families blessed. We pray for them because it is a matter of love. We need to see that every part of our lives is fulfilled. It will keep us from competing with others spiritually, financially, economically or in any other way. Prayer exists where love abides. If we love others, we will pray for them.

Prayer is also thanksgiving. If we are grateful, we will not complain. To complain means that we are charging GOD with mishandling our lives. We are saying that it is all GOD's fault, and He should have planned something different for our lives. GOD says He **knows the plans that He has for our lives**, and unless He reveals the plans to us, we do not know the plans. Only if we continue in prayer will He tell us.

Prayer is communication with the Father. We speak, He listens. He speaks, and our hearing is dull. He speaks constantly, and we must be able to hear. We need to not only hear what he said yesterday, but we must hear the proceeding word of GOD. If we miss what GOD has spoken, will He repeat it?

Abraham set out on a journey, and he did not know where he was going. Every step that he made was an affirmation of what he heard GOD saying to him. Abraham did not second guess GOD. He had established a relationship, and he knew the voice of GOD. He did not confer with the flesh to make sure it was GOD speaking. I imagine that if Abraham had not heard God directly and precisely, then he could have climbed the wrong mountain. If Abraham had climbed the wrong mountain, I am sure that we would have a different account of the story documented.

If we cannot hear what GOD says, will He continue to speak? We must develop an effective means of communicating with our Father otherwise we risk missing valuable information that will allow us to obtain, maintain and progress in the abundant life.

When we pray, we also make requests to GOD. GOD knows all things, and He knows what we want as well as what we need. When we pray, we are asking for the things we desire from GOD. We do not ask because our neighbor has something similar, and we want to boast about how much better our thing is compared to theirs.

We have not because we ask not and GOD will not give it to us if we **ask a miss**. If we covet what others have, we forfeit our request. We are using GOD to compare and that is not what a loving Father will allow us to do. He is not partial. He does not love one child more than the other. He may trust one more than the other because of our faith level and our obedience. If we want to have what others have so that we can compete or compare, GOD is not honored by that.

Prayer is not a "give me" tool. It is not a "please bless me better" tool. It is a form of communication that keeps us in the right standings with our Father. It is a tool for direction and for effectively completing our destiny on earth. GOD is the giver of every good and perfect gift.

Whatever we need, we can obtain from GOD. We do not need to compare what others have or what we do not have. We need to love GOD and others and that will cause us not to compare our lives with others. If we stay on common ground, we become one. We should be striving to be as one instead of placing the flesh out there as if it is so important. There is one Lord who is for us all and who wants to abide within us all.

Prayer is also a means of confession. **If we declare a thing, it shall be established.** Jesus told His disciples to **speak to the mountain**. Now the mountain can be anything. When He said to speak to it, he was saying make confession to it. Say the thing that we want to happen. If we speak life, then life will appear. If we speak death, then death is pronounced and will manifest.

Confessing is speaking that which is in the heart. Our prayer of confession is our confidence. That which we have confessed will happen. And with faith, we wait for it.

Father, I pray that all prayers are filled with faith and are declarations of positive confessions. I pray that all will have a wonderful prayer life filled with thanksgiving. I pray that each prayer is mixed with faith and that we believe we receive whatsoever we pray for. I pray that we will all obtain the faith of Abraham, our father of faith, who said that **"he was fully convinced that whatever YOU promised YOU are more than capable to perform it."** *In Jesus' name, Amen.*

Confess

We speak words every day, and we are not aware that those words are confessions. If we say one day I will be rich and believe when we speak it, it will happen. **Jesus said you shall have whatsoever you say (Mark 11:22)**. If we say words with "to death" on it, we are making a confession. For example, when someone says our children are worrying us "to death", we confess that worrying will kill us.

We must be mindful of what we say. Words come out of the abundance of the heart. The mouth will speak those words that are in our hearts, and we will be making confessions that we may later regret. If we do not humble ourselves by putting ourselves under subjection to GOD and have Him to cleanse our hearts, we may be confessing our own destruction.

The word confession is made up of two words. **Con** is **"to direct the steering of"**, meaning to guide in the way it should go, and **fess** which is **to own up to**. Con also means **to commit to memory**. When we confess, we are guiding what we say in the direction it should go, and we commit it to memory. Therefore, if it does not happen immediately, it will happen sometime later. Con also has negative associated meanings such as **one who persuades by deception, a convict or one who is in opposition or disagrees with**. Another negative meaning is **a trick**.

When we confess, we are steering our spoken words in a direction that will produce life or cause death. Confessions make life exciting when we are positive and make life miserable when we are negative.

There are times when bad situations occur, but the practice of positive energy causes even the worst situations to have a brighter outcome. The outcome of any situation can be changed by the words that are spoken during the circumstances. Whenever we speak, we must be careful to use words that will uplift, edify, and encourage not only others but ourselves as well. We must continue to be positive in an unlikely situation. If our words are to be positive and full of life, we must have a heart that is positive. The scripture says that **out of the abundance of the heart the mouth speaks.** That means that if the heart is bitter, then bitter words will come out. If the heart is sad, sad words will be spoken. If the heart is glad, glad words will be spoken. **O generation of vipers, how can ye, being evil, speaks good things? For out of the abundance of the heart the mouth speaketh (Matthew 12:34).**

The scripture also says that death and life are in the power of the tongue. **Death and life are in the power of the tongue: and we that love it shall eat the fruit thereof (Proverbs 18:21).** Positive words are words of life, and negative words are words of death. We must be careful what we say. We can kill someone with negative words, not physically, but spiritually, mentally, and emotionally. We never know how powerful our words are. Our words can heal or kill. We can cause someone's life to flourish, or we can damage someone for life just by the words we speak.

Confession is the path that gives directions to our journeys. The road to our destiny is mapped out by the words we speak. If we confess that we can never do anything right, the outcome will be that we never do anything right. If we confess that we are successful and everything will work out all right, the outcome of that confession will be just what was said.

It is a concept that seems so easy that most people do not believe it. So, we continue confessing negative words. We never realize how bad the situation really gets until we change our confessions.

Confessions can motivate and inspire someone to be a famous inventor or writer, an astronaut, a scientist, a doctor, or a lawyer. Or confession can be the tool that manifests a bum, a dope addict, a drunk, a loser, a thief, a friend, or an enemy. We need to be careful that we do not accept what others say about us. For instance, if a parent confesses that a child is stupid and worthless, it will not be so until that child believes the confession. If the child has a confession of his own that he believes (even if it is contrary to what the parent has confessed), then once he confesses what he believes about himself, the child will be what he has confessed. On the other hand, no one can make a confession about us if we are not in agreement with that confession. Only when we believe what has been confessed about us will it begin to manifest.

If we believe the words we speak about ourselves and others, those words will have power and will determine the directions of our lives. To confess means we will speak with conviction that which we believe is true. If we confess that we will walk to the store, then we will get up and walk to the store. If we confess that we will get an A on an upcoming test, we will believe enough to prepare to make an A on the test. If we confess that we will fail a test, then we will not prepare, and we will fail the test.

Confession and belief go together. If what is spoken is not believed, then it will not manifest. It is the belief that causes confessions to manifest. Belief will keep the confession alive. When we believe that we are destined to be great, we will continue to confess it. If we believe that we are worthless, we will continue to confess what we believe about ourselves, and therefore, the fruit of the confession will manifest. We must begin and continue to make positive confessions about our lives and not allow others or ourselves to continue to confess negative things into our lives.

Confessions are necessary to attain greater things in life. When we meet someone who confesses what we will do, we immediately doubt the outcome. Whenever there are innovative ideas, people will begin to say that is impossible. They say that has never been done before. They will list all the negative reasons why it will not work. But sometimes the very thing that has not been done is the very thing that we are destined to do.

We need others to be more encouraging and speak life into us, to stand with us in our positive confessions. Everyone would want the same if it was them making confessions that seemed unimaginable or impossible. No matter what others say if we have a confession that we believe to happen in our lives, then we must not let the nay-sayers convince us otherwise.

Confessions are sometimes for future outcomes that may take decades to manifest, but if the confession never changes, it will happen. Noah made a confession of rain. Noah believed GOD. He heard God, and he obeyed

GOD. If Noah had not believed GOD, he might not have had positive confessions. He may have ignored the possibility of rain and never would have built the ark. Thank God Noah was able to hear and believe God. He had never seen rain before, and neither had anyone else. It took one hundred and twenty years for the manifestation of rain to appear, but Noah kept his confession alive by faith and by preparation. It was his belief that caused him to continue to confess that it was going to rain. It was the belief in his confession that made him work to build an ark to protect his family from the unknown manifestation of rain. He did not know if it was hot or if it was cold. He did not know if it was wet or dry. He only knew that he had a confession and he believed it.

The Wright brothers invented the airplane and had a confession. The person who invented the automobile had a confession. And the person who invented electricity had a confession. Not only did they have a confession, but they had a belief in their confessions. Our confessions are life, and it is up to us to never give up on our positive confessions.

Confessions are an act of faith, and we must believe with all our hearts that every confession will happen. GOD who is our strength and our helper **will do exceedingly and abundantly more than we can ask or imagine Him to do (Ephesians 3:20).**

Confession is tied to faith. When we confess, we are demonstrating our faith level. With patience, we wait for the results. Confessions are seeds sown. The word of GOD declares that **whatsoever we sow; that shall we also reap (Galatians 6:7)**. Our positive confessions are good seeds for the soul and produce a prosperous harvest, whereas negative confessions are detrimental seeds to the soul and produce negative, unripe fruit.

We must be careful not to compete, complain or compare. We must confess the changes that we want to see in our lives. Confession is making a claim. With the words we speak, we lay the foundation for our future. If we continue to speak words that line up with death, then our future will be built on that foundation. But if we speak words that line up with life, our future is bright, promising, and rewarding. Confessions come from the heart because **"for out of the abundance of the heart the mouth speaketh" (Matthew 12:34).**

We must be willing to live a life of confession. We make confessions all the time. I will see you tomorrow. I will come over to your place. I will go to work today. I will call you tonight. These are all confessions.

Confessions are words spoken of an event that will happen presently or futuristically; confession is admitting a statement as truth. If we confess the truth to any situation, the outcome will be true. If we confess that **"no weapon formed against us shall prosper" (Isaiah 54:17),** then we live our lives invincibly and without fear.

Thank YOU, Heavenly Father, for YOUR word that records so many promises that we can confess. We declare that we will no longer walk in comparison of others because we are **co-heirs with Christ** *and we have everything that Christ has. We confess that* ***all things work together for our good and no weapon that is formed shall prosper against us.*** *We thank YOU for being* ***so loving and kind*** *to us. As we walk in YOUR will and are led by the Spirit of GOD, we will receive our inheritance. We walk in the boldness of the Spirit to confess that* ***we have everything that we need.*** *We seek to obtain YOU and the fullness of YOU because if we obtain YOU, we obtain all things.* ***For in YOU are all things.*** *We believe by faith that we are who YOU say we are. In Jesus' name, Amen.*

Citations

"Thought." *Webster's II New College Dictionary*, 2nd Edition, Houghton Mifflin Harcourt, 1999, page 1147.

"Compete." *Online Etymology Dictionary*, Dictionary.com. www.dictionary.reference.com/browse/comete. Retrieved February 14, 2004.

"Rival." *Merriam-Webster Dictionary*, Merriam-Webser.com. ww.merriam-webster.com/dictionary/rival. Retrieved February 14, 2004.

"Compare." Dictionary.com. www.dictionary.reference.com/browse/compare. Retrieved Feb. 1, 2008.

The Holy Bible, KJV and GNV versions.

(Political campaigns) Negative campaign ads during presidential election.

Simkin, Penny, et. al. Pregnancy, Childbirth, and the Newborn: The Complete Guide. Meadowbook Press, 1991.

www.lifeascentcoaching.com/index.htm (Marc Fey), May 2003.

Hill, Napoleon Hill. *Think and Grow Rich*. Ralston Publishing Company. 1937, page 102.

Borowitz, Eugene B. & Frances Weinman Schwartz. *The Jewish Moral Virtues*. Jewish Publication Society, 1999, page164.

Malbim, Meir Leibush. Malbim on Mishley: The Book of Proverbs in Hebrew and *English*, translated by Charles Wengrov and Avivah Gottlieb Zornberg, Feldheim Publishers.1993.

Fohrman, David & Nesanel Kasnett, Nesanel, editors. *Babylonian Talmud Volumes 2 and 3*, 1999.

Damazio, Frank. *The Making of a Leader*. City Bible Publishing, 1988, page 119.

"Con." Dictionary.com. www.dictionary.reference.com/browse/con. Retrieved February 1, 2008.

"Confess." Merriam-Webster's Dictionary of Law Merriam-Webster, Inc. www.dictionary.reference.com/browse/confess. Retrieved February 1, 2004.

"Confession." Merriam-Webster's Dictionary of Law Merriam-Webster, Inc. www.dictionary.reference.com/browse/confession. Retrieved February 1, 2004.

"Fess." Dictionary.com. www.dictionary.reference.com/browse/fess. Retrieved February 1, 2008.

"Determination." Collins English Dictionary - Complete & Unabridged 10th Edition. http://dictionary.reference.com/browse/determination. Retrieved December 13, 2009.

"Impacts on Aquatic Species." *Hurricanes: Science and Society,* The University of Rhode Island,https://hurricanescience.org/society/impacts/environmentalimpacts/aquaticimpacts/?fuseaction=ShowRelatedLinks#references.

About the Author

Melvina Bryant is a dedicated individual with a diverse range of experiences and interests. She has had a love for writing since early childhood. Melvina is a songwriter and poet. She has a degree in Computer Science and a long-standing career in the telecommunications field. Melvina is currently an App Developer Release Manager, a realtor, and an actress, demonstrating her versatility and passion for various pursuits. Melvina is also the owner of Pooh Polly's Beauty Station, a beauty supply store dedicated to providing personalized attention and inclusive products tailored specifically for Black women.

Melvina is a mother and a grandmother. She is a person who sees a need and tries to meet the need. Melvina is a spiritual person who has a strong faith in GOD. Her involvement in teaching Sunday school reflects her commitment to giving back and helping others. She desires to help young people and to make a positive impact on others. Melvina's future aspirations are to be a tool for the success and well-being of others.

www.ingramcontent.com/pod-product-compliance
Lightning Source LLC
Chambersburg PA
CBHW050657160426
43194CB00010B/1980